SMARTER
CHARTERS

ALSO BY CHRISTOPHER CASWELL:

The Basic Book of Boating
Championship Dinghy Racing
Trailerable Sailboats

SMARTER
CHARTERS

Christopher Caswell

St. Martin's Press   New York

SMARTER CHARTERS. Copyright © 1994 by Christopher Caswell. All rights reserved. Printed in the United States of America. No part of this book may be used or reproduced in any manner whatsoever without written permission except in the case of brief quotations embodied in critical articles or reviews. For information, address St. Martin's Press, 175 Fifth Avenue, New York, N.Y. 10010.

Production Editor: David Stanford Burr
Designer: Judith A. Stagnitto

Photos by Christopher Caswell unless otherwise stated.

Library of Congress Cataloging-in-Publication Data

Caswell, Christopher.
    Smarter charters / Chris Caswell.
       p.   cm.
    ISBN 0-312-10550-9
     1. Sailboats—Chartering. I. Title.
    GV811.C37 1994
    797.1'24—dc20   93-43022
                              CIP

First Edition: March 1994

10 9 8 7 6 5 4 3 2 1

This book is dedicated to Rhea, who taught me that tiny umbrellas in the drinks and some decor with dinner can vastly improve even the worst chartering weather. She doesn't travel light, but she does travel well.

CONTENTS

THE BASICS

What's It All About?	**3**
Choosing a Charter Area	**18**
Choosing a Charter Company	**24**
Selecting a Boat and Crew	**34**
Paperwork	**51**
Powerboat Charters	**61**
Crewed Charters	**69**
What to Take	**81**

THE SKILLS

Seamanship	**91**
Anchoring	**100**
Navigation	**111**
Dinghies	**117**
Safety and First Aid	**123**
Provisioning and Cooking	**136**
Living Aboard	**147**

CHARTER AREAS

Caribbean	**159**
Bahamas and North America	**174**
Europe	**191**
South Pacific and Asia	**205**

Charter Companies	**221**
Further Reading	**225**
Magazines	**230**
Checklists:	
Clothing and Gear to Take with You	**232**
Bareboat Checkout List	**235**
Daily Checklist	**237**
Location Index	**239**
Topic Index	**245**

THE BASICS

WHAT'S IT ALL ABOUT?

It was a pristine morning—clear and bright, with the promise of an afternoon breeze to balance the sun's warmth. Padding quietly up the companionway ladder into the cockpit, I settled back against a cushion and wiggled my toes with pleasure on the cool teak deck. Just off our stern, small waves rushed up the white-sand beach with a soft shushing sound, and the green palms sparkled silver with dew in the faint tropical breeze.

A rich man at play? Hardly. This was simply another morning aboard a charter yacht, anchored in a quiet cove that could be anywhere in the world. Where the pleasures of Tahiti, the Virgin Islands, and the Mediterranean coast were once the private playground of the wealthy, today's yachtsman can sample any of them on an average vacation budget.

The first myth that must be dispelled is that chartering a yacht is an expensive proposition. In fact, the price is comparable to what you might expect to pay at a good resort hotel, but with pleasures that only a yacht can provide.

As an example, let's look at a 38-foot yacht in the British Virgin Islands. This particular yacht, typical of those available at many charter companies, has two separate cabins, two private head compartments, and a dinette that converts into another double berth, giving a total sleeping capacity of six adults. For the sake of this comparison, let's say that because you want maximum privacy, only two couples are going to charter this yacht together.

In the January-to-April high season, when most visitors schedule their vacations to escape the winter chill of northern climates, the yacht costs about $2,900 per week, or $1,450 per couple.

A good resort hotel would charge at least $200 per night in the same area, so the basic cost is essentially equal. In a hotel, however, the meals are a major additional factor in your budget. A basic resort breakfast can easily run $10 a person (and that isn't for room service), while sandwiches, salad, and wine for lunch can exceed $15. A week of simple meals in a hotel can cost more than $350 per couple, which is far more than the cost of provisions aboard a charter yacht.

In a hotel you have the choice of waiting in line for a seat in the dining room or splurging on room service. Aboard your yacht, you can choose between a meal alfresco with a spectacular view, or take breakfast back into your cabin for a lazy morning. Even if you leave the yacht to dine ashore every evening, your total vacation costs will be lower than in the resort hotel. So what's holding you back?

You'll have a wide latitude of boats to choose from, and we'll look at the various types and some of the decisions you'll make later in this book. For the meantime, however, the chart on pages 16–17 will give you an idea of what you can expect to pay for various-sized yachts in different charter areas around the world.

The price of a charter yacht is directly proportional to the quality and maintenance level of the yacht, the season, and the size of the charter company. Larger charter operations are able to keep their prices down because of their buying power and because their on-site staff reduces the cost of routine maintenance as well as any necessary repairs. A one-boat charter company is likely to be more expensive for the same reason.

Types of Charters

Before you sign up for a charter, you'll need to decide which style of charter best fits your needs. In general, there are six different types of yacht charters:

1. Bareboat
2. Crewed
3. Flotilla
4. School
5. Special-interest
6. Head boats

These aren't hard and fast categories, and as the charter industry expands worldwide, you're more likely to find combinations and even new gimmicks to entice you. Let's take a look at the six basic types.

Bareboating

Bareboat charters are the most popular, and you'll find fleets of bareboat charter yachts worldwide. "Bareboat" doesn't mean clothing optional—it means that the yacht is supplied to you without a crew. You and your crew will operate the yacht, doing everything from hoisting and trimming sail to anchoring at day's end. You do the sailing, cooking, and cleaning. All the challenges, and all of the rewards, are yours.

On a bareboat charter you'll be able to decide where to go each day, when to anchor, and when to linger. On the other hand, you'll be assuming responsibility for the yacht, so you'll need to exercise both skill and caution in your actions.

But don't let that scare you off. Each charter company carefully checks you out on the boat, assessing your skills as the staff shows you how everything works on board. You'll probably be asked to take one of the staff for a spin around the harbor to check you out on your boathandling skills as well.

Before you leave the dock on your first day, you'll get an

extensive briefing that will answer all your questions about the sailing area. Using charts like those supplied on your boat, a member of the charter company team will show you the best anchorages, hazards to watch for, and provide details on everything from weather to sightseeing to restaurants.

Bareboating has become an alternative to yacht ownership for many former boatowners, who found the expenses of maintaining their own boat year-round outweighed the pleasures. As one experienced bareboat sailor noted, "Bareboat chartering is like being a grandparent . . . you get the pleasures when you want them, for as long as you want them, but with none of the responsibilities!"

Besides, the average boatowner has neither the time nor the money to sail over the horizon to faraway places. With a bareboat charter, he can board a jet to Tahiti, Thailand, the French West Indies, or the Greek archipelago and set sail immediately. As one bareboater pointed out, "I'm simply sailing around the world . . . one piece at a time."

Crewed Charters

While most people think of crewed charters as the province of "Lifestyles of the Rich and Famous," that simply isn't the case. For every 175-foot mega-yacht that is chartered by jet-setters for $20,000 a day with a full complement of uniformed crewmembers, there are dozens, even hundreds of 50- and 60-footers run by husband-wife crews that can be chartered by people of modest means.

In the simplest form of crewed chartering, only a skipper joins you aboard your boat. At most bareboat charter companies you can hire a skipper to help you learn the ropes or explore an unfamiliar area. After a day or two, the skipper departs, leaving you to enjoy a bareboat charter for the remainder of your vacation. Depending on the cruising area, the rate for a short-term skipper can range from $50 to $125 a day, plus the cost of the skipper's return transportation to the starting point.

For many charterers, having a professional skipper aboard relieves any worries about navigation, anchoring, docking, or the myriad little stresses of being entirely on your own. At the same time, a skipper can provide a valuable introduction to a new cruising area, giving a sense of security for future bareboat cruises in the same area.

A second form of crewed charter involves taking along a professional cook to handle all the galley chores. Every charter company provides you with a choice, usually ranging from a Cordon Bleu–trained chef to a local cook who takes pride in preparing regional fare. The cook handles the shopping, cooking, serving, and clean-up for your meals, but you're on your own for keeping the rest of the boat tidy.

By far the most common crewed charter is the husband-wife team that operates its own yacht as a full-time business. In most cases, the husband is the skipper, while the wife acts as chef, hostess, and deckhand.

In this situation, you'll usually be allowed to do as much or as little as you choose, leaving the boat's handling to the crew or taking an active part. The crew prepares the meals, working from a menu agreed upon beforehand, and usually handles the physical work such as anchoring, launching the dinghy, or furling the sails.

While the skipper may veto an idea because of danger, you'll be allowed to choose when and where you go—dallying in spots that you enjoy and upping anchor from those that you don't care about.

Flotilla Charters

The flotilla charter is an idea that began in Europe and has now spread to charter fleets worldwide, although you'll still find far more flotillas scheduled in the Mediterranean and Aegean than anywhere else.

A flotilla charter is a group cruise of several charter boats, usually similar in size or speed, shepherded by a mother ship with a professional captain from the charter company. This is the "buddy system" of boating. In some flotilla charters the individual boats are free to sail alone during the day, choosing their route and stops but anchoring together at an agreed-upon harbor each night. Other flotillas sail as a group, sometimes having races between the boats, but always staying within sight of each other.

A flotilla is a comfortable combination of bareboat and crewed chartering. The people on the other boats can provide advice, camaraderie, and any needed parts or repairs as the trip progresses. It's obviously less stressful on each skipper, since the mother ship keeps an eye on the flock, and it's an excellent way for those with limited sailing experience to acquire new skills in a controlled environment.

Most flotillas have a predeparture briefing for the crews each morning, led by the professional skipper, who covers the day's route as well as sights and hazards in the area. With a conventional bareboat charter, the briefing covers an entire week or more, which is often hard to absorb. The flotilla concentrates on one day at a time.

A flotilla charter may also get better moorings as a group, and the charter company often has more clout in local harbors, with easier access to dinner reservations, groceries, and sightseeing tours.

The negative side to a flotilla charter is that you aren't as free to plan your own itinerary, and must work with a large number of people to agree on all the details. Flotilla charters are often used by yacht clubs or other groups with similar interests.

I recently enjoyed a flotilla charter through ATM Yachts in Tahiti, using three Beneteau 51s and a Privilege 48-foot catamaran as the mother ship. Ours was a loose arrangement: we agreed each morning on where we would rendezvous that day, and amended our plans by radio as weather or personal inclinations changed.

On some days, we sailed from island to island in solitude and gathered aboard the catamaran in the evening for cocktails and socializing. Other days, we would agree to meet at a particular *motu* (islet) for swimming and lunch before proceeding at our own pace to the night's anchorage. The crewmembers aboard the catamaran, with their local knowledge, were able to suggest the best beaches, coves, and restaurants, but the other crews were free to decide what they really wanted to do. I found this system a pleasant way to explore a new area without worrying about charts, weather reports, or guidebooks.

SAILING SCHOOLS

Relatively new in chartering are the packages offered by sailing schools, which combine the pleasures of bareboating with a learning experience to improve your skills. These are usually flotilla charters, sometimes with a mother ship but more often with a skipper/instructor assigned to each boat.

Each school structures its program differently, but most start with a classroom session that covers the area to be sailed as well as details about the local weather. Once aboard the boats, each crew is responsible for running the boat itself under the guidance of the instructor, who steps in only when necessary. The crews rotate positions to learn the intricacies of steering, docking, anchoring, navigation, and even cooking aboard.

Usually the only requirement for such a course is knowledge of the basics of sailing, since the purpose of the trip is to learn the skills necessary for future bareboat charters. At some schools, a seven-day cruise might end in an overnight solo trip with the skipper following along in another boat.

Sailing schools are an excellent way for people with small-boat experience to upgrade their skills in larger cruising boats. Most schools offer a diploma or certificate at the end of the course, and since they are usually operated in conjunction with a charter company, the certificate is often accepted as a substitute for sailing experience when planning a bareboat charter with that company.

A certificate does not give you carte blanche, however, and you'll still be expected to demonstrate your skills to the satisfaction of the charter company before it turns over one of its bareboats to you.

SPECIAL-INTEREST CHARTERS

Because a bareboat charter is such a good way to explore a region in depth, many charter companies combine sailing with one or more other areas of interest to attract devotees of both.

You may, for example, find a skin-diving charter package that includes a flotilla of bareboats as well as a mother ship complete with certified dive instructors, air compressors, and all the other necessities of a skin-diving expedition.

Educational charters are common in Europe, incorporating an intellectual pursuit into a cruise with a guide aboard. In the Greek islands, for example, a number of charters are available for those with an interest in archaeology. Either a crewed charter or a flotilla with a mother ship will sail between sites of interest, and an archaeologist in the group serves as a guide and lecturer on the subject.

For those who prefer animal life, the Galapagos Islands are becoming a popular destination for crewed charters that include a naturalist to explain the unusual creatures found in this region of the Pacific.

The Sunsail charter company has set aside certain flotilla cruises in the Mediterranean for singles, allowing crews to meet other sailing-minded singles aboard as many as a dozen yachts.

Nearly any subject that you can dream up, from wine-tasting to French cooking, fishing to bird-watching, can be (and has been) the basis for a charter. In many cases these are conceived and exe-

Most charter areas can provide spectacular souvenirs of your cruise, such as this shell collection.

cuted by a charter company, but there's no reason that you can't gather a group of friends with similar interests and put a charter package together on your own.

Head Boats

These are a combination of a bareboat and a crewed charter, often packaged by a bareboat charter company. In essence, you simply reserve a single berth on a charter boat, where you will be joined by others doing the same thing. If you enjoy making new friends and don't have enough people to put together a charter crew of your own, this is the way to go.

The Moorings, for example, offers a "Cabin 'n Cruise" package that puts six guests aboard a 50-foot yacht, and Sunsail has "Stowaway Holidays" for singles and couples. A captain is on board to handle the responsibilities, and guests share double cabins. You'll do the crew work, just as on a bareboat, and you'll have a say in where to go and what to do, but without having to assemble an entire group on your own.

Getting the Most from Your Charter

If you're an enthusiastic supporter of packaged tours in which the tour operator herds you on and off the bus at each hotel and sight, then you won't be happy on a charter. A successful charter doesn't just happen. Like any vacation, it requires a certain amount of planning and preparation.

Can You Sail?

The basic prerequisite for bareboat chartering is that you know how to sail or, in the case of a powerboat, know how to operate such a yacht. Charter yachts, regardless of size, are valuable and you'll be responsible for the safety of the vessel and crew, so you should have a good working knowledge of boating. Bareboat chartering is not for the rank amateur, and you'll need to have both sailing ability and some cruising experience before you cast off on your own.

The skills you'll need, however, depend upon where you plan to charter. In the British Virgin Islands, for example, there are few underwater hazards, no fog, and the sailing area is just thirty-six miles long, so you navigate by eye rather than relying on chart skills. Tackling a more challenging area, however, requires more than rudimentary sailing and boathandling skills.

Don't try to skate by with marginal skills, because charter companies are expert at ferreting out imposters with a sailing questionnaire and a test on their boat. You can avoid a lot of grief, as well as a possibly ruined vacation, by being coldly analytical about your own abilities beforehand.

On the positive side, don't be put off if you have experience with small boats instead of yachts of charter-boat proportions. If you sail centerboard boats regularly, you'll have a good feel for sailing even if you're weak in big-boat handling, which you can pick up quickly in many of the milder chartering locales.

To encourage new charters, companies such as The Moorings

A Moorings 50 thunders along a reach in the Caribbean, showing that charter yachts aren't necessarily slow. (Photo courtesy The Moorings) will provide you with a skipper for two days to get you started on your charter and to make sure you understand everything necessary. The only additional cost is the return fare for the skipper to his base of operations.

It's also important to have decision-making experience aboard boats of similar size to your charter boat, in addition to time as a crew member. Simply sitting as "deck fluff" doesn't qualify you as a skipper.

Gaining Experience

There are several ways to gain the experience and skills necessary for bareboat chartering: sail locally with friends, take courses at a sailing school, sign on for a flotilla charter, or sail as crew on a charter.

If you're interested in sailing, you're probably friendly with boatowners, and now is the time to ask for their help. They know how difficult it can be to learn sailing, and nearly every skipper is glad to help novices. Under their supervision, practice docking and anchoring, or see if they'll let you be the "skipper for the day," with responsibility for all aspects of the day sail. While this is the most convenient and least expensive way to learn to sail, it isn't always the best. Some friends or family members may not have the skills or patience to teach others to drive, and the same holds true in sailing.

In many cases, your best choice is to sign up with a sailing school, which generally will have a wide range of courses from basic sailing through celestial navigation. In between, you're likely to find courses in anchoring, boathandling, and basic navigation to help hone your charter cruising skills.

Plan Ahead

The starting point is to be perfectly honest about your level of experience. If you've skippered cruising yachts for years, then you're probably able to handle a charter anywhere in the world. If your nautical résumé is closer to novice level, then you should select both the boat and the cruising waters more carefully, opting for a simple boat and relatively protected locales.

Using your chartered yacht as a classroom, a sailing instructor quickly can teach you the skills you need to venture out on your own.

Other chapters in this book will cover the details of choosing a charter company and the particular yacht, as well as selecting the cruising area, but advance planning is the key to the success of your trip.

Most experienced charterers derive as much pleasure from the preparation for the trip as they do from the cruise itself. Investigating the charter companies, scouring the guidebooks to decide upon an area, and making lists of provisions and gear are all a part of the charter experience.

Choosing your crew is equally important, and many an otherwise delightful charter has been ruined by a crew that was incompatible. On the other hand, I've had less-than-perfect charters that were saved because the crew laughed rather than argued, and were willing to bend rather than snap. Don't take a chance on chartering with people you don't know well.

Instead, assemble the crew from people with your own interests, tastes, and enthusiasms. Living together in a relatively confined space for a week can bring out the worst, and the best, in anyone. Careful crew selection is a prime consideration.

WHAT TO EXPECT

Like everything in life, a charter is going to be exactly what you make it. I know of people who have gone off to the most exotic locales, sailed through incredible scenery, and returned home bemoaning the high humidity.

On the other hand, I enjoyed a delightful charter in Scotland where wind and rain were the one constant from the minute we boarded the boat. But my memories are of a warm cabin with good friends, an exciting thrash to windward with spray flying, watching a squall approach from atop a ruined castle, and shrugging off my foul-weather gear in front of a pub's roaring fireplace.

I've had mirror-flat calms during charters in Baja California, and again in Thailand, and most of my cruises in the Pacific Northwest have had their share of rainfall. Neither calm nor rain has detracted from the pleasures. Snuggling into a warm bunk while the rain patters on the hatch overhead is an exquisite toe-wiggling luxury, and swimming in midocean from a becalmed yacht is a unique experience.

If you expect the weather always to be perfect, the food to be gourmet, and the seas to be calm, then you're likely to be unhappy whether you're on a charter yacht, a cruise ship, or at a five-star resort.

Those who get the most out of charters are the people who remain flexible, who are willing to change their plans on a whim or with the weather, and who believe that getting there is less important than enjoying the trip.

When packing your duffel bag for a charter cruise, leave your expectations at home. Open your mind and your spirit, enjoy what you can, and take home memories of incredible sunsets, pristine beaches, and afternoon sails on sparkling waters.

16 The Basics

Sunset over a charter yacht off Thailand's Phuket coast.

Sample Charter Rates

The following list gives a range of rates for varying sizes of boats in the various charter areas. High and low rates indicate seasonal differences.

Boat	Size	Locale	Sleeps	High Season	Low Season	Company
Freedom 30	30'	British Virgins	6	2940	1960	Bitter End
Nonsuch 30	30'	British Virgins	4	1820	1155	NorthSouth
Catalina 30	30'	Pacific Northwest	6	900	710	Penmar
Beneteau 32	32'	British Virgins	6	1890	1050	Sunsail
Oceanis 32	32'	Greece	5	1890	945	Kavos
ATM 32	32'	Tahiti	4	2020	1660	ATM
Oceanis 350	34'	Bahamas	6	2653	1400	Sunsail
C&C 34	35'	British Virgins	6	1960	1295	NorthSouth
Ericson 35	35'	Pacific Northwest	5	1100	865	Penmar

Boat	Size	Locale	Sleeps	High Season	Low Season	Company
Islander 36	36'	Pacific Northwest	6	1240	965	Penmar
Moorings 37	37'	Baja California	5	1961	1258	Moorings
Crealock 37	37'	Pacific Northwest	6	1400	1085	Penmar
Moorings 38	38'	British Virgins	6	2912	1603	Moorings
Baltic 38	38'	Maine	6	2100	1890	Sun Yacht
Moorings 38	38'	Tahiti	6	2380	na	Moorings
Moorings 38	38'	West Indies	6	3059	1680	Moorings
Beneteau 38	38'	West Indies	6	3003	1743	Sunsail
ATM 392	39'	French West Indies	5	2740	2180	ATM
Privilege Cat	39'	West Indies	8	4500	2875	Privilege
Baltic 40	40'	Greece	6	3600	na	GPSC
Moorings 432	43'	Tonga	7	2744	na	Moorings
Oceanis 430	43'	Turkey	9	3605	1960	Kavos
Oceanis 430	43'	U.S. Virgins	9	3195	1895	Caribbean
Irwin 44	44'	Bahamas	8	2590	1942	Eleuthera
Freedom 44	44'	Pacific Northwest	7	2010	1545	Penmar
Sunsail 445 Catamaran	45'	Bahamas	8+	4995	2995	Sunsail
Morgan 46	46'	Pacific Northwest	8	2225	1705	Penmar
ATM 474	47'	French West Indies	8	3980	2780	ATM
Swan 46	47'	West Indies	10	5450	4150	Nautor Swan
Privilege 48 Catamaran	48'	U.S. Virgins	8	6500	5000	Privilege
Moorings 500	50'	British Virgins	10	4921	2709	Moorings
Oceanis 500	50'	Greece	9	4900	3430	Kavos
ATM 515	50'	Tahiti	9	5400	4500	ATM
Oceanis 500	50'	U.S. Virgins	9	3995	2495	Caribbean
Beneteau 500	50'	West Indies	10	5166	2842	Moorings
Centurion 49	50'	West Indies	9	4300	3400	Jet Sea
Moorings 500	50'	West Indies	10	4921	2681	Moorings
Moorings 51	51'	Baja California	8	3409	2126	Moorings
Irwin 52	52'	West Indies	8	4295	3650	Sunsail
Jeanneau 560	56'	Greece	10	6000	na	GPSC

See page 221 for details on charter companies.

CHOOSING A CHARTER AREA

*C*hoosing the area for your charter can often be the trickiest part of your adventure, because so many variables come into play. You'll need to review your preferences, your skills, your budget, and your flexibility to make an educated decision on a charter location.

One starting point is to read the many boating magazines, both in the United States and abroad, that focus heavily on the growing chartering market. Many experienced charterers build files of magazine clippings on various areas for reference when they start their decision-making process.

Be aware, however, that all boating magazines are enduring hard times, and as their advertising income from boat manufacturers dwindles during the ongoing slump in the marine market, charter advertising is increasing as this segment of the business continues to blossom. For this reason, you'll see more articles about chartering than ever before. Keep in mind that magazines are supported by advertising dollars, and it is often difficult for the editors to bite the hands that feed them. In more than two decades in the boating-magazine business, I have seen only a handful of fearlessly critical charter stories, while I've also waded through countless stories that fawned over companies, boats, and areas that I wouldn't recommend to an enemy. Take anything you read with a grain of salt.

One strength of the boating magazines, of course, is the sheer magnitude of charter-company advertising. Take advantage of the toll-free numbers of many companies to ask for their brochures and promotional materials, which you can use to start narrowing down the areas that interest you.

Your own location is obviously the starting point for deciding where to take a charter vacation. If you live in the Caribbean, then you can probably eliminate that region from your short list. Charter industry statistics suggest that the vast majority of charterers travel more than 1,000 miles to reach their destination, a large number will go 3,000 miles, and there is a growing segment that is willing (time and airline fares notwithstanding) to travel to another hemisphere for their charters.

Climate

One of your first general decisions will be the climate that you prefer. If you dislike cold, then you might want to eliminate many of the northern charter cruising areas of Europe and North America, which can be brisk even in midsummer. On the other hand, if the tropics are too steamy for you, skip parts of the South Pacific, Asia, or lower Caribbean. Bear in mind, of course, that not every area has the same weather throughout the year, and you can often find a season that is acceptable. For example, the Pacific Northwest is temperate in the summer, cool in the spring and fall, and downright cold during the winter.

Time of Year

Your sailing vacation may or may not be dictated by a specific vacation schedule, such as during Christmas or Easter holidays, or during times convenient for your own business. But you should narrow in on your charter window early in your planning, so you can avoid wasting time on areas that are simply unsuitable. If summer is your only getaway time, for example, you can quickly rule out Baja California, where the summer heat and sun can be unbearable. On the other hand, summer is the ideal time to explore the Apostle Islands of Lake Superior.

The chart on page 22–23 outlines the preferred sailing seasons for a number of different areas, but always bear in mind that weather is one variable that is beyond your control.

Boating Experience

Once again, you need to be brutally honest about your level of boating expertise. Areas such as the Virgin Islands and the Bahamas are appropriate for the novice charterer, with generally protected waters, short distances between anchorages, and predictable weather with good forecasts.

You'll need a far higher level of skill to tackle chartering in the Hebrides Islands off Scotland, where tidal currents swirl around shoals and rocks. The weather can change suddenly, and good harbors are few and far between.

The wind and water aren't the only factors that make an area more challenging. Foreign waters mean foreign languages, unfamiliar charts, and social customs that compound the normal problems faced by a charter crew. Before you set sail on the coast of Norway or navigate through the shoals of Belize, be sure of your own skills.

What Can You Afford?

Nobody likes to talk about money, and too many otherwise lovely charters have been felled by a shortage of funds. Once you've set aside a certain amount of money that you're comfortable spending on a vacation, make sure that your planned charter can stay within that budget while still leaving a safety margin.

The cost of the bareboat charter is the major expense, and is easily determined from the charter company's advertising materials. Add to that your airfare or other transportation costs to and from the charter company base. Don't forget all the seemingly minor related costs that add up, such as airport taxes, meals in transit, taxis or buses, and even fees for overweight baggage if you plan to bring extra gear.

Provisioning is the next major expenditure and, depending upon the area, you may prefer that the charter company handle it at a flat rate per day or from a checklist of supplies. Leave slack in the food budget, though, because you'll surely want to dine ashore occasionally. Besides, even in the most remote areas, I've never been on a charter where we didn't buy food to augment our provisions as we went along. In Baja California, we couldn't resist the lobster and jumbo shrimp offered by the local fishermen. In Tahiti, a few bottles of red wine always turned up in the dinghy after forays ashore. In Scotland, every little village had a bakery with mouth-watering pastries that became absolutely necessary to top off the next meal.

Finally, ask the charter company for a list of other specific expenses that their customers encounter, which might include fishing licenses, fuel for the dinghy or bareboat, mooring fees, harbor fees, document fees (if you cross international borders), or any of the other "nickel-and-dime" costs that can break your carefully set budget. One surprise for many crews is a value added tax applied to charters in British or French waters. The French tax (AVT) is 7.5 percent of the charter cost, figured on a daily basis for each day spent in French waters, and can add several hundred dollars to your budget.

Also check on fuel, cooking gas, and water. Some companies include these items in the package cost, while others provide you with full tanks at the start of your cruise and then charge you to top them off at the end. In some areas, fuel can be quite expensive and water nearly as precious, so you should understand the policy of your company.

No matter how badly you want to do a particular charter, if it is close to exceeding your budget, you should probably find a less expensive charter that won't leave you constantly worrying about money.

Other Considerations

Obviously, climate, time, experience, and budget are the keys to choosing a charter location, but don't overlook other likes or dislikes. If your idea of a pleasant vacation is to have dinner at a different restaurant every night, then you should pick an area (such as the Mediterranean) where you can do exactly that. If you want to get away from the bright lights and don't care if you see anyone for days on end, pick your charter region accordingly.

Are you a fisherman? Find out what fish are biting, and when, before you sign up for a fishing-oriented charter.

Do you speak a foreign language and want to practice? While English is spoken on any waterfront, the locals in a country speaking your second language will be delighted to help with your efforts to converse.

Picture your prospective charter vacation in your mind. Do you see yourself in solitude or do you want nightlife? Does your spouse rebel at the idea of cooking and want to be served? Do you prefer empty harbors or do you like meeting people in busier anchorages?

Charter Seasons

The following chart shows the chartering areas around the world, as well as the best season for cruising.

Location	Best Season	Comments
North America & Caribbean		
Bahamas	December–March	June–September has high humidity; strong northers blow January–April
Baja California	November–May	Summer is very hot, fall is hurricane season
Caribbean	Mid-December–March	The best winds are April–July; hurricanes possible July–October

Location	Best Season	Comments
Chesapeake	Mid-April to October, with spring and fall best	Midsummer has light winds and thunderstorms
Florida	January–May	June–September is hot and humid
Great Lakes	June–September	Crowded in July
Maine	June–September	August is foggy
Northeast	May–October	Light summer winds
Pacific Northwest	June–September, spring and fall best	Crowded in midsummer
Sacramento Delta	May–October	
Southern California	Year-round	Crowded in summer
Europe		
British Isles	May–September	Expect rain
Greece	Spring and fall	Crowded in summer; *meltemi* winds blow regularly
Mediterranean	April–October	Summer months are crowded with tourists
Northern Europe	May–September	Expect rain
Scandinavia	May–September	Long daylight hours
Turkey	Fall and spring	Summer is hot and windy
Pacific & Asia		
Australia	May–October	Summer is wet and unstable
French Polynesia	March–November	November–April is humid and warm
New Zealand	Year-round, but high season is October–May	June–September is windy and cooler; December–February is crowded
Thailand	November–April	Summer is typhoon season, humid and rainy
Tonga	April–November	January–March is hurricane season

CHOOSING A CHARTER COMPANY

*J*ust as important as picking the right area for your needs is choosing the right charter company. Without putting too fine a point on it, the boating business has always attracted large numbers of dreamers and schemers, and the charter business is no different.

Like the very best waiters, a good charter company is nearly invisible, making sure that everything goes smoothly but without fuss. It picks you up at the airport and ferries you directly to your boat, where all your provisions are ready, the boat is clean and inspected, and your departure briefing is comprehensive but understandable. When you return, the boat is checked in quickly and you are soon on your way home.

A bad charter company (and make no mistake, there are some) can turn the best planned vacation into a frustrating and costly disaster. Even seemingly unimportant things can make a major difference. On one Bahamas charter, we noticed a distinct odor to our boat that we couldn't quite place. It wasn't until one of our crew became ill that we discovered that the charter company had decided to paint our auxiliary engine the morning of our charter. Our sick crewman was severely allergic to paint fumes, which reappeared every time we ran the engine.

On a Caribbean charter (with a company specializing in top quality racer-cruisers), we arrived late one night to find that our van driver didn't know where our boat was, nor could he find any of the staff who did, and we didn't know the name of our vessel. Already exhausted after a long flight, we stood around in the heat until someone finally arrived to find our assigned boat. The following day, the company discovered during our checkout that the anchor windlass didn't work. It couldn't repair the windlass until the next day, so we lost one charter day chafing in frustration with nothing to do.

There are more than a few horror stories about bankrupt charter companies disappearing with everyone's deposits, or crooked companies that schedule you for a particular yacht and then, upon arrival, claim that boat is broken down and insist that you take a smaller or less acceptable substitute instead.

But most bad charters are the result of small things going wrong, such as a necessary repair that can't be done until the following day, a refrigerator that fails far from the nearest market, or worn-out equipment that is obviously patched together.

The large charter companies have grown by making sure that their customers go away happy enough to tell others about the experience. Many small companies remain small for the opposite reasons. Lest this sound like an indictment on a basis of size alone, I should point out that I have chartered quite happily with small companies whose personalized service is superb. But until you have a wealth of experience under your belt, it's generally best to stick to the larger fleets.

Large charter companies, like big car-rental companies, have several advantages. First, they usually standardize their fleet to certain types of boats, and in some cases may even have the yachts built to their own specifications. That makes maintenance easier for the shore crews, and it allows the stockpiling of spare parts for emergencies. In addition, a company with similar boats can quickly substitute an identical replacement in case the yacht you chartered is out of service.

Second, large companies have the ability to send out service boats in case you have problems during the cruise, which is beyond the scope of a small mom-and-pop operation. Penmar Marine in the Pacific Northwest, for example, not only has a service staff on

A fleet of yachts awaits charterers in a Caribbean setting.

duty twenty-four hours a day with a chase boat, but also maintains a four-place aircraft to fly spares quickly to charter boats in more distant areas.

Where to Look

But where do you start when looking for a charter company? The best place is with the major boating magazines, such as *Sail, Cruising World,* and *Sailing* in the United States, or *Yachting World* and *Yachting Monthly* in England.

In addition to the monthly advertising pages for charter companies, these magazines also produce special sections on chartering in their fall issues (August is often popular), which include editorial material on various charters and comprehensive directories of charter companies by area.

Charter brokers (which advertise in the above magazines) are in a unique position, since they often represent a multitude of charter companies worldwide. The broker's fees are paid by the charter company, not the client, so your costs remain the same. Every reputable broker takes the time to visit the various charter sites and actually examine the boats, so you can get good advice on boats and locations that best suit your needs.

Talk to several charter brokers to see if you develop a rapport. Find out if they have personal knowledge of the boats they represent, and if they have chartered in the areas in which you have an interest. Ask for recent references from your broker, preferably for similar boats in your chosen location.

It won't be long before you have a stack of brochures and folders from the charter companies. Use these just as a stockbroker uses an annual report to determine the strength of a company. Don't forget that numbers can be juggled, so this is just the starting point in your detective work.

With any service-oriented business such as chartering, length in business is generally synonymous with quality of service: the good companies survive while the bad ones fail. Unfortunately, the bad ones don't always fail quickly enough.

If you aren't sure how long a company has been in business, go through back issues of boating magazines at the library and see if it has been advertising for at least five years. After you have more chartering experience, you'll be more capable of making your own decisions as new companies spring into operation.

In reading the literature and the magazine charter directories, you'll soon see how many boats are in the fleet of each company. I'm generally wary of any company with fewer than eight boats. There are exceptions, of course, particularly in remote locations that may not be able to support more than a few charter boats, or when there are extenuating circumstances, such as a resort hotel with a small but well-maintained fleet.

Keep in mind that many companies have several locations. A thirty-boat fleet at five widely spaced bases falls in the small-company category: they can't easily substitute boats, they probably don't maintain full stocks of spare parts at each base, and the number of service personnel is reduced at each location as well.

Questions to Ask

Cruising Limits

Ask about the cruising limits for each charter base. The charter company is likely to set specific boundaries as the outer limits of your charter, whether because of international borders or hazards. If you have a specific destination in mind, make sure to ask if it is included in its cruising area. Most Virgin Islands charter companies, for example, specifically exclude the island of Anegada for their customers because of its distance from the island chain as well as the underwater hazards surrounding it.

Age and Maintenance

Another factor to check is the vintage of the boats. A charter boat, no matter how well maintained, is subjected to heavy usage. Fiberglass boats, regardless of what manufacturers claim, will simply wear out. For years, The Moorings retired every boat after four years of charter service, the time they had determined that their boats started to show their age. Recently, however, The Moorings has added a separate class of charters called the Value Line, which uses five- and six-year-old yachts moved from regular service. Since many of the previously retired yachts from The Moorings wound up as the basis for other charter fleets, the Value Line yachts are aimed at economy-minded charterers who might otherwise have gone to these smaller companies. In this way, a charterer gets a reduced rate without having to give up the service and reliability of a larger company.

Some charter companies buy up the older boats that have been dropped from service with the large charter fleets, and you'll find them advertised using the name given by the original company, such as the CSY 51. Once again, use extra caution when considering an older boat.

Maintenance is a prime factor, since even the best boats need to be carefully serviced. In the large fleets, a boat may charter thirty-five or more weeks a year, which is a grueling regimen for even the finest construction. Ask about the maintenance proce-

dures, which gives you some insight into what you can expect.
At a minimum, there should be a twenty-four-hour turnaround time between charters, which allows for cleaning and repair of any minor problems. Stay away from charter companies whose boats come in at 10:00 A.M. and go out again at 3:00 P.M.

At ATM Yachts, for example, each boat has a noon-to-noon service period after very charter. After every ten weeks of charter service, each ATM yacht is taken out of duty for ten days, during which time it receives major maintenance, ranging from engine tune-up to the complete disassembly of anchor and sheet winches. Any necessary parts are replaced and, as with most major companies, ATM automatically replaces certain parts and systems after a certain period of use.

Be sure to ask about the breakdown policy of the charter company. Does it accept collect phone calls or does it monitor VHF on a daily basis? If not, you'll be stuck making expensive phone calls to get things fixed. Find out how it handles repairs, too, since some companies have their own service boats, while others may ask you to have the repairs done by outside contractors.

While you're examining the boats, keep in mind that some charter areas have predominately company-owned boats, while other areas are under a lease-back or management relationship. In the Caribbean, for example, the larger companies either own the boats outright or have them on such a tight management program that the owner has literally no right to use the boat unless he makes a reservation. In the Pacific Northwest, on the other hand, the charter companies rely on a more flexible management system, allowing the owner to do his own maintenance, keep the boat at his own dock, and use the boat whenever it isn't booked for a charter. For just that reason don't expect to see a look-alike fleet neatly lined up in the Pacific Northwest.

DEPARTURE AND ARRIVAL TIMES

Each company sets strict hours for the departure and arrival of its boats, geared to allow sufficient time for cleaning, restocking, and repairing each boat before the new crew arrives. In some cases, these departure times can effectively cut a day off your cruising time. One company, for example, sets noon as the end of a charter, but they include the postcruise check-in as part of your cruising time. While they make every effort to minimize the time it takes to complete the return procedure and inventory (including sending a staff member out to greet you offshore and start the process), the check-in time still counts as part of your cruise. If you arrive only a few minutes before noon, you may be charged extra since your inspection will extend past your return time.

The result is that you are obligated to spend your last night within a short distance of the charter base so you can return the boat early in the morning. By the same token, some companies will not release the boat until 6:00 P.M., which almost forces you to stay aboard the first night at their base unless there is enough daylight left to get to a nearby anchorage. Keep both the departure and arrival times in mind as you plan your cruise itinerary. Check your contract, which should stipulate the penalties for late return, regardless of whether it is one hour or six hours.

Credit Checks

Articles in various magazines often tell readers to ask for a bank reference or a Dun & Bradstreet rating from their prospective charter company, but that seems foolish to me. First, any reputable banker is hardly going to tell a casual caller that Charter Company X is about to go bankrupt, even if he is aware that it has less than $100 in its account. At the same time, the number of major companies in all types of business that have fallen to recessionary woes despite good D&B ratings makes me cautious about putting too much faith in such a rating.

While your friends and acquaintances can't put your mind to rest about the financial stability of a charter company, poll them when considering various companies. The boating world is surprisingly small, so it's not unusual for a friend to pass you along to someone you don't know, but who has valuable information.

The "Old Boy Network"

Because all charterers face the same fears about charter companies and charter areas, a rather remarkable underground information service has sprung up. Someone in your yacht club knows someone at another club who chartered with the company in question, and is usually more than happy to discuss all the pros and cons at length. To tap into this information source, you need to start asking questions. Don't limit your investigation to friends, but feel free to drop the question at the local marine hardware store, at a nearby sailmaker, or even place a cold call to the commodores of yacht clubs in your area. You'll be surprised by the amount of assistance you get.

Your best bet for a bareboat charter is with a company that does nothing but charters. A wonderful Bob Newhart comedy routine a number of years ago revolved around a decrepit airline company called the "Grace L. Ferguson Airline and Storm Door Company," which is quite similar to some charter companies today. You may find yacht brokers who also run a small charter fleet out of their marina, usually with boats that are for sale, but these are often ill maintained because their primary business is selling boats, not vacations.

Remember that Avis and Hertz don't run driving schools, they just rent cars. The fewer things your charter company is trying to do, the more it can concentrate on you as a charterer. Stay as far away from the boatyard-brokerage-charter companies as you would the Ferguson Airline and Storm Door Company.

As you review the literature from the various companies, you might want to make a chart that compares the boats, features, and prices. The charter business is extremely price competitive and most companies have rates that are within a few dollars of each other, but you'll occasionally find one that is either much more or much less expensive. In either case, it's worth your trouble to find out why.

A more expensive charter might include equipment with the basic charter fee that other companies list as optional, such as an outboard for the dinghy, a spinnaker, or a Windsurfer. A less

32   THE BASICS

Although spinnakers usually are not included as standard charter equipment, they can provide extra speed and excitement on a breezy afternoon.

expensive charter may reflect similar shortages which are then balanced when you compare identically equipped boats. Don't be afraid to ask the company about the reason for the difference in price, however. It may be offering a special discount for a particular season or boat, and any reputable company should be able to defend a higher price as well.

Last but just as important as any other item in selecting a company is asking for a list of references. Again, reputable companies have nothing to hide and can usually supply you with names and phone numbers. You should get at least three recent references (people who have chartered within the last month), and you should ask specifically for other charterers from your area. That not only minimizes your telephone costs, but also provides some assurance that you aren't calling relatives of the charter-company owner.

As I mentioned before, an unwritten code among charterers

virtually guarantees you honest and detailed answers to your questions. Be sure to call all the references with a list of questions in front of you.

Sailing Schools

Sailing schools have also entered the charter market in recent years, usually as a sideline to instruction. Obviously, the sailing school is in the business of selling instruction, and some prospective charterers felt they were being strong-armed to take some classes before being allowed to charter the boats.

If you do need instruction, however, this might be the best choice, because the company will know your skills and be more likely to charter a boat to you after you take its course. Your best bet is an organized sailing school rather than a course offered by a resort as part of its package. Be sure to get a detailed description of the course. Have a clear understanding of how much classroom work is involved, how many days and nights are spent on board, and what type of boat is used.

Ask about the instructors, who should have Coast Guard licenses, and find out about their résumés and sailing background. Last, see how many students are included in the class, and whether that is a comfortable number for the intended boat.

As a minimum, a cruising course should include instruction in boathandling, anchoring, docking, and navigation.

SELECTING A BOAT AND CREW

*S*electing a charter boat is an inexact science at best, since it relies so heavily on personal preferences and abilities. While I'm not antisocial, my basic tenets are that bigger boats are better than small boats, and a small crew is better than a large one. Take my recommendations in this chapter with those tenets in mind.

First, it's useful to look at the charter market and see how it has evolved. Until the mid-1960s, charters might better have been termed "rentals," because the boats were essentially privately custom-built yachts that were rented out for a week at a time. The arrival of fiberglass revolutionized the charter business by creating identical boats in great numbers, so you are now likely to arrive at a charter base and find dozens of sailboats distinguishable from one another only by their names.

The first of the modern large charter companies began when New Jersey dentist John Van Ost came up with the fleet concept and gathered a group of other professionals to launch Caribbean Sailing Yachts (CSY). They started with a handful of 30-footers that they placed in the British Virgin Islands in 1967. As the business blossomed and the concept was accepted, CSY commissioned the Carib 41, a center-cockpit two-cabin yacht that was a novelty in American waters. Caribbean Sailing Yachts owned their first boats outright, but later sold boats to individual owners who then turned them over to CSY on a lease-back arrangement. This provided each owner with a fixed monthly payment without any responsibility for upkeep, mooring fees, or insurance. The arrangement also gave CSY complete control over the boats, so they were able to provide a high level of maintenance and reliability.

The Moorings, founded two years later by Charlie and Ginny Cary, started in a similar fashion with a six-boat fleet of Pearson 35s and is now the largest charter company in the world, with hundreds of yachts at more than two dozen bases worldwide. The company has expanded into hotels and resorts, crewed yacht charters, sailing and scuba-diving schools, and a comprehensive owner/ management program for the yachts that are now built to Moorings specifications.

Jumping into the fray are numerous European-based companies, such as ATM Yachts and Sunsail, which learned the trade in the Mediterranean and have now also established bases worldwide.

As the charter fleets were initially established, the boats were essentially production fiberglass sailboats from U.S. companies such as Morgan and Gulfstar. Because of the decline of the American sailboat business, most of the new charter yachts are coming from European companies such as Beneteau and Jeanneau.

The early boats were often less than stellar performers, and many of them could barely slog to windward at all, relying on their auxiliary engines when the wind was in an unfavorable direction. These boats were also spartan inside, with vinyl bunk cush-

This vintage fiberglass charter trawler is perfect for one couple to explore the Bahamas.

ions, a smattering of pots and utensils, and cubbyhole head compartments.

Today, however, a modern yacht is not only fully equipped, but also luxuriously outfitted. Using an inverter to convert DC power into household current, some yachts feature microwave ovens, blenders and food processors, electric toasters, TVs and VCRs (with a videotape library), compact disc stereos, and even hair driers. It's not exactly man against the elements, and such amenities may be what you're trying to escape on your cruise, but there's no denying the pleasures of a slushy daiquiri in the cockpit after an afternoon sail.

Performance as well as comfort has improved in modern charter yachts. Older boats were heavy, beamy, and carried too little sail to make them even marginally exciting, while modern designs are light, lean, and fully rigged for lively sailing. Cruising spinnakers are often an optional accessory. If you want extra performance during your charter, be sure to inquire when booking.

General Considerations

Two factors tend to govern the choice of the boat: number of crew expected and cost. Taking fewer people on a larger boat obviously increases the cost per person, but (in my mind) not enough to discourage the idea. I'd rather spend a few dollars more to ensure a level of luxury than spend an already expensive week wishing I had a larger boat. It's often a good idea to leave one bunk free. There always seems to be an overflow of gear that needs a place to be stored, and an extra berth is a good place for it. This also leaves a little flexibility in the sleeping arrangements, so someone can move if they prefer another bunk.

Ability is another factor to consider. You must be able to handle your boat in all conditions, including anchoring, docking, and sailing in strong winds. Four people can handle a modern 50-foot charter yacht easily, but it would be too large for a couple alone, who would be better off with a 40-footer.

Size

Size of the charter boat is a starting point, although different layouts can make a 35-footer seem like a 40-footer or, unfortunately, vice versa. The charter company literature will suggest a suitable number of people for each boat although, once again, you need to be wary. Study the accommodation plans for each boat, count the number of berths and cabins, and see if this layout seems reasonable for your crew. If you plan to take three couples but the boat has two staterooms with double berths and two single bunks in the main cabin, one couple is never going to be happy about the arrangements.

A larger boat gives you the space to spread out as well as the maximum level of privacy for everyone. (There is, of course, a point of diminishing returns when the boat gets too big to handle easily.) Many boats have a forward and an aft cabin, each with a double berth and usually with a private head and shower for each

The aft cabin on this sailing yacht has an island-style queen-sized berth, settee, and extensive storage.

cabin. There may also be a dinette table that converts into a double berth in the main salon, but my recommendation is to keep that purely for dining and entertaining. I sailed aboard a charter recently where one extra person was sleeping on that dinette/berth. In the evening, there was always a bit of crashing about as the berth was transformed and, in the morning, the reverse process had to take place before breakfast. Because the main salon was being used as a bedroom, the rest of the crew had to retire whenever the odd man wanted to sleep, and we had to tiptoe around in the morning until he awoke. It made a 40-foot boat seem cramped.

As you peruse European charter brochures, however, remember that there is more of a "bunkhouse" mentality overseas and an attitude that if there is room to sit down, then there must be room to sleep. North Americans tend to prefer more elbow room, and I think that six people need a minimum of two heads, two showers and, preferably, three private staterooms.

There is a rather unique difference between American and European charter sensibilities that I discovered recently during a sail in French Polynesia. Our crew encountered a French group aboard a 32-footer that had four berths in two cabins and a single head, yet there were seven aboard the boat. At night they were sleeping on deck and, if it rained, they were stacked on the cabin floor, yet they were having a marvelous time.

Layout

The charter brochures will provide you with drawings of the layout as well as photographs of the interior, and a little eyeballing will give you a good idea of the boat interior.

In many charter fleets, you may have to choose between an aft cockpit and a center cockpit layout. With an aft cockpit the steering is done from near the stern; the cockpit is located well aft on the boat. A center cockpit, on the other hand, is usually raised above the cabin, placing the steering nearly amidships. Both layouts have their advantages and disadvantages.

Since the center cockpit is located farther forward, it is closer

Selecting a Boat and Crew 39

(Above) This center-cockpit Swan features a permanent bimini top to shade the crew under sail.

(Below) This charter yacht features a spacious aft cockpit with twin steering wheels and a permanent dining table, as well as a platform on the stern with folding swim ladder, freshwater shower, and storage for gear.

to any spray coming over the bow and therefore is likely to be wetter. On the other hand, this layout allows for a private and spacious aft cabin, and generally offers more interior room than an aft cockpit yacht of similar size.

An aft cockpit is somewhat drier, and doesn't involve as much climbing up and down to get to the deck. An aft cockpit yacht tends to have better performance, because of less windage and because designers often make compromises in favor of cruising comfort in a center cockpit yacht.

Catamarans

Relatively new in Caribbean and Pacific charter fleets are the catamarans that have been accepted with such fanfare in Europe. Catamarans are a different breed from conventional sailboats.

In general, a catamaran is not only faster but also roomier than a similarly sized monohulled sailboat. A 48-foot catamaran, for example, has four large staterooms (one forward and one aft in each hull) that are well separated for privacy, as well as a spacious salon and galley in the deckhouse spanning the two hulls. The salon may have comfortable seating for a dozen or more people, while the cockpit may seat two dozen more easily. Many catamarans have twin steering wheels so the helmsman has a good view from either side of the boat, and twin engines are the normal power.

With the thin hulls offering minimal resistance, a catamaran is easily driven under either sail or power, often cruising at more than the top speed of many monohulls. Knifing through the water creates less spray, and the big net "trampolines" between the two bows are a wonderful place to sprawl and watch the water flash past. On one Tahitian catamaran charter, a school of dolphin played just inches away from us.

A second feature of the catamaran is stability, since the widely spaced hulls counteract the leverage of the sails. Most catamarans rarely heel more than 5° in normal conditions, so it is a good boat for anyone worried about "tipping over." On the other hand, the catamaran is light for its size, so it has a shorter and quicker sailing motion that some sailors dislike.

Selecting a Boat and Crew 41

(Above) Catamarans such as this Privilege 48 offer speed, stability, and extensive deck space. They also accommodate more people than single-hulled boats of the same size.

(Below) Anchored for the night, this yacht has an additional awning over the boom to provide sun protection for the deck area, and in areas where evening sprinkles are common, it also allows the hatches to be left open.

Another feature is the shallow draft, which allows some catamarans to anchor in water shallow enough to walk ashore, although you always need to be careful of rudders and propellers.

Catamarans take getting used to, since they react slowly to the rudder and have large turning radiuses compared to monohulls. Anyone with experience in a similar size sailboat, however, can quickly make the transition to catamaran sailing.

Ventilation

It's difficult to tell from the brochures whether a boat is claustrophobic inside, or even if it has enough ventilation to be habitable on muggy evenings. You might want to start making notes on various boats of interest, and check them out at a local boat show or even at a dealership. But keep in mind that many of these interiors are changed, often in major ways, for the charter companies.

Aside from the number of berths and heads, ventilation is the most important factor in a good charter yacht. There must be a good cross-flow of breeze, in all conditions. Aboard a Beneteau 51 recently, I found it almost impossible to sleep when we weren't able to open all of the hatches in the torrential rains at night.

I also spent a grim night in the Bahamas many years ago. It was steamy down below but I rigged a windscoop for the hatch over my head and was rewarded with a cool flow of air—until it started to rain and my windscoop became a waterfall. Frantically I dismantled the funnel, and the rain promptly stopped. For the next hour, I struggled with the same up-down Laurel and Hardy routine until I gave up and fell into an exhausted (and damp) sleep.

One way to check the ventilation is to simply count the number of opening portholes, hatches, and vents in the brochure photos. The more the better.

Water

Another precious commodity aboard a charter yacht is water, because you and your crew will probably not use it sparingly. This is, after all, a vacation and not a forced march. In many charter areas, water is also an expensive commodity, and you can find yourself paying a dollar or more a gallon to replenish your tanks. Two showers, plus an on-deck rinsing nozzle for swimmers, can quickly drain the tanks on an average yacht, so make sure there is enough to go around. By the same token, having a saltwater faucet in the galley can ease the onboard drought if you use it to wash dishes, following up with a freshwater rinse.

As a guideline, Sea Recovery, a company that makes reverse osmosis watermakers, suggests that ten gallons per day per person is sufficient on yachts under fifty feet for showering and domestic chores. A naval architect noted for cruising designs reckons that an economical shower takes about two gallons, washing up in the galley takes another two gallons, and activities like shaving, brushing teeth, and washing hands take another gallon, for a minimum of five gallons per person per day. For comparison's sake, then, a four-person crew needs between twenty and forty gallons per day and a six-person crew needs thirty to sixty gallons per day.

Using those numbers, it's interesting to check the water capacity on various boats. The Moorings 45f5, for example, has four showers for a three-cabin yacht but only 152 gallons of water. The Moorings 432, also with three staterooms, carries 230 gallons, while the Moorings 500 (with permanent berths for eight) carries 400 gallons of water. At Sunsail, the Endeavour 51 (with three double staterooms) has 450 gallons of water, and its Grand Banks 42 trawler, also with three staterooms, carries 350 gallons. On any boat you'll need to conserve water, but it's more critical on some boats than others.

Privacy

Yachts are obviously not built like homes, so take into account whatever level of privacy you have in mind. If two staterooms are next to each other with no intervening lockers or heads, then assume that the sounds in one cabin will probably be audible in the other. Look for layouts that put a stateroom at each end of the yacht and use the main salon, galley, and heads as a sound buffer in the middle.

This may seem a minor point or draw snickers from those who imagine the sounds of whoopee echoing through the boat, but noise can become a point of real irritation on a week-long cruise. After all, how many of you have spent the night separated by only a piece of thin plywood from an adjoining cabin with someone who is even a moderate snorer? And how do you know if your prospective crew snores?

Sailing Gear

Nearly every modern charter yacht relies on roller-furling headsails to simplify sail handling. While they're not the latest in racing sails, they will greatly simplify your charter. Some charter yachts use various types of furling mainsails, but any type of workable sail-handling system that reduces the effort or manpower required is a boon on a charter.

Cruising spinnakers usually cost extra, but they can turn an otherwise ho-hum sail into a more exhilarating afternoon with the added boat speed that they generate, not to mention their colorful designs. Cruising chutes are attached to the bow and use no spinnaker pole, so they are easier and safer to use than conventional spinnakers, but they still provide increased performance.

Anchor Gear

The luxury of an electric anchor windlass is often overlooked until you have to up anchor in deep water, and then it goes near the top of the checklist for every sailor looking at potential charters.

The length of the anchor rode and the amount of chain will be different for varying areas. In the South Pacific, all-chain anchor rodes are common, since they offer protection from chafe on the coral reefs. In other parts of the world, however, you may be using a combination of chain and line. Your boat should have at least one stern anchor or spare along with sufficient rode to moor the yacht if something happens to your bow anchor.

Selecting a Boat and Crew

(Right) This sailboat galley is located in the passageway to the aft cabin, allowing the cook to brace comfortably when the boat is under way. The drawbacks are that the cook blocks the passage and may find the motion uncomfortable without windows.
(Above) This compact galley nearly surrounds the cook, with a gimballed stove/oven, double sink, and cupboards for dishes.

Galley

The galley must be large enough to handle the dining needs of the entire crew, as well as any guests you may invite aboard. If you're feeding a large crew, you might want to make sure the galley is large enough for two people, so you can invite a helper to share the work.

The refrigerator/freezer should have the capacity to store a week's worth of goodies. Some charter companies can provide additional ice chests for any over-supply. Most charter yachts have mechanical refrigeration systems driven by the engine, but a few of the smaller boats rely on blocks of ice. Find out what to expect ahead of time, because ice can be a problem in a tropical climate.

Equipment

The equipment list for each yacht is a major variable, and each company approaches the gear question differently. Some assume that you can pick the items you want from a list of extras, while others simplify their operation by putting everything on board.

In every case, a good bimini top is a starting point for any sunny climate. Look carefully at the photos of the yachts in the brochures, as the size of these tops varies widely. Some cover only about half of the cockpit, leaving the helm area as well as the forward end of the cockpit completely unprotected. That means that the helmsperson will always be in the sun, and you won't be able to stretch out in the cockpit with your back against the cabin, either. The bimini should also be usable when under sail, not just when powering or anchored.

The charter area also imposes some variables on the standard equipment. Sunsail, for example, provides outboard motors as standard equipment for the dinghy in the Caribbean, but not in the Mediterranean where more time is spent in marinas than at anchor. Rigid dinghies are supplied in the Caribbean (to withstand the constant beaching on rock and coral), while inflatables are used in the Mediterranean to conserve space since they aren't used as often.

Cockpit cushions are another nicety that can make a great difference in crew comfort. You'll be sitting in the cockpit while

This yacht has a folding bimini top to protect the helmsman from the sun, but doesn't offer much shade for the rest of the cockpit. The outboard motor mounted on the stern pulpit provides safer storage than on the dinghy.

sailing, and sitting in the cockpit at anchor, so you'd better be comfortable. Some charter companies list "teak seating or cockpit cushions" on the standard equipment list as though they were the same, but I'll take the padding anytime. Ask before you go.

The only entertainment aboard charter boats in the past was whatever local station you could find on the radio. Today, you're likely to find a complete stereo system as a minimum, and many yachts also have televisions, cassette and disc players, and video libraries. Bring your own tapes or discs of favorite music, because you can't rely on the selection found on board.

Choosing Your Crew

The military spends considerable time and money screening candidates for its submarine and bomber crews, as well as anyone who will be sent to a remote outpost, but most charter crews are assembled among friends at the yacht club bar.

For once, the military minds are right. Six people on a 40-footer for a week is a breeding ground for emotional conflicts. Stir in some bad weather and you can reach the flashpoint quickly. A small crew gives everyone more personal space and relieves the conflicts of waiting to use the head, dining in a crowd, or even finding places to stow gear.

In choosing a crew, personality is the best starting point. Try to sail with people who have a ready sense of humor and a relatively mild temper. Too many little things can (and do) go wrong aboard any boat that you have to simply grin and bear it.

A nonstop talker can be an abrasive element, especially if you value quiet time and want to curl up in the cockpit with a good book. A "Chatty Cathy" or "Talky Tommy" can dim the beauty of the most outrageous sunset.

By the same token, personal habits can also make or break a cruise. If you're not a smoker, descending into a cabin filled with a blue haze will grow old quickly. Even smokers who are considerate enough to smoke only on deck (and to leeward) carry an aroma with them that can set off an avid antismoker, and most charter companies that assemble crews for flotillas will designate certain boats as smoking or nonsmoking.

Drinking is another consideration. Charter cruises can lead to startling discoveries, however: The mild-mannered friends who sip wine at your home during dinner can turn into sloppy drunks on their vacation time, and it's sometimes hard to anticipate these problems.

"Common interests" doesn't just mean that you all enjoy Ludlum novels (although being able to share books on a cruise is a real asset!). It also includes your outlook and expectations. Some friends of mine chartered with another couple and, too late, discovered that the other twosome wanted to go ashore and party every night. There was a constant conflict between having dinner aboard or ashore, as well as allocating the use of the dinghy for an entire evening. It also meant that one couple was always pushing to reach the next harbor in time for happy hour ashore, while my friends would have preferred to leisurely explore new coves and anchorages.

Varied levels of skill can be a factor or not, depending upon the people. I've sailed with crews of absolute novices who were challenged by learning to sail but who maintained their humor throughout any crisis. I've also sailed with crews of highly experienced sailors who squabbled constantly about everything from sail trim to anchoring procedure.

As a general rule, there should be at least two experienced sailors aboard every charter, as a hedge against emergency. Every so often I hear stories of charter boats circling helplessly after the skipper fell overboard, because no one in the crew knew how to start the engine or even radio for help. This may be a moot point, however, since most charter companies share this concern and expect a minimum level of competency from other crewmembers.

By the way, relatives fall into exactly the same category as all other crewmembers, and you should be prepared to include or omit them for all the same reasons. Just because you are related to a person doesn't necessarily mean she or he will fit into a charter situation and, in some cases, that relationship is a hindrance.

Professional charter boat crews sometimes mention a CFH (Crew From Hell), but there is also the PC (Perfect Crew), who will have most, if not all, of the following traits on a bareboat charter:

1. They offer to share the cost of fuel and food without being asked.
2. They don't arrive with six pieces of hard-sided Samsonite luggage, but instead have no more than one large duffel bag.
3. They bring a selection of paperback books, which they share with the rest of the crew.
4. They don't understand boredom.
5. They respect quiet time and privacy.
6. They eat what is prepared for them by others.
7. They share the cooking and cleaning chores without being asked.
8. They don't monopolize the helm and, conversely, offer to help sail the boat.
9. They are tidy and put away their personal gear, especially

when they are sleeping in a common area of the boat.
10. They leave the head compartment cleaner than when they entered.
11. They bring their own suntan lotions, snorkel gear, and seasickness remedies.
12. They don't monopolize the dinghy, or take it ashore and strand the crew.
13. They volunteer to help with the hard work, such as raising sail or hoisting the anchor.
14. They take and offer advice gently and calmly.

PAPERWORK

Booking the Charter

Once you've made your decision about the boat, the location, and the specific time you want your charter vacation, it's time to make the reservation.

Most companies have a toll-free phone number, and the operators will have either the master charter book or the same information on a computer. You'll usually start with the date and the location, followed by the boat type, and they can quickly check on availability for you.

In some cases, they may not have the exact dates you want, and will ask if you can move your arrival or departure dates one way or the other by a few days. The specific boat may also not be available, in which case they can recommend an acceptable substitute.

Each company varies in its policies, but some are willing to negotiate a reduced price on a larger boat if the one that you requested is unavailable, so be sure to ask for a discount if that is the case.

Once you've come to an agreement on the date, location, boat, and price, the charter agent will hold your reservation for a set period, usually from ten to fourteen days. During that time, the company will send you an information packet with a written confirmation, which should outline all of the details agreed upon by telephone and include a sailing experience questionnaire for the skipper and each crewmember to fill out.

An invoice for your deposit will also be in the packet and, again, each company varies in its policies. Some require a 50 percent deposit to hold the booking. Others ask for 25 percent at the time of the reservation, with another 25 percent due ninety days prior to the charter and the remainder due thirty days beforehand.

THE CHARTER QUESTIONNAIRE

Every charter company will send you a questionnaire regarding your experience as well as that of other members of the crew. It uses this to make sure that you're capable of being turned loose in the charter area of your choice. You'll need to return this questionnaire with the other paperwork as you book your charter and, more than anything else, this questionnaire will decide your chartering fate.

In most cases, you will be asked about previous charters and specifically about those where you were in command. The company will ask whether you own a boat, its size, and in what areas you normally sail. It will want to know if you've cruised (or raced) outside your home waters before, and you'll also need to indicate your navigational experience.

Every charter company has stories of skippers whose questionnaires made them sound like America's Cup winners but who, in person, barely knew one end of the boat from another. In some cases these imposters have been allowed to hire a skipper for the duration of their charter but, in some instances, have simply been refused the charter, losing a portion of their deposit in the process.

A more honest approach by a young couple with basic sailing skills (but no navigational experience) had better results. The charter company, upon reviewing the couple's questionnaire, realized these first-timers were requesting an area that demanded more than their abilities. A company representative called them and tactfully suggested they might have a better time in a less demanding area. They agreed, spent a wonderful week sailing with no problems, and have now been chartering twice a year in progressively more challenging areas to build up their skills.

Transportation

In many cases, charter companies will also arrange your transportation to and from the charter base. They often can get you a better price on airfares than your own travel agent, simply because they buy "blocks" of airline seats for boats full of arriving charterers.

Try to arrive at least one day before the charter is due to start. This allows some slack in case of missing luggage and missed or delayed airline flights, not to mention a chance to catch up on jet lag. I don't much fancy setting out in an unfamiliar but expensive yacht through foreign waters, particularly feeling as I have after getting off a fourteen-hour flight through six time zones.

It's also a good idea to book flights that either are open ended, or allow you to change the return trip for a minimal fee. This permits you to stay an extra day if you choose, and if there are boat problems, you can make up the time at the end of the charter.

While many charterers routinely ship their duffel bags, I prefer to put my bag inside a hard-sided suitcase and ship it with protection. I don't want to break anything inside the duffel, and the airlines are notably cavalier about dropping suitcases onto softer luggage. A hard suitcase also provides security against theft and water damage if it's left on the runway at small island airports in rainstorms when the ground crew takes shelter.

A final word about luggage: Check your baggage through to the last major airport in your itinerary, and then hand-carry it onto the small commuter airline yourself to make sure that you and your baggage arrive at the same time.

As a photographer, I prefer not to have any of my film X-rayed, so I empty all my film canisters out of their cardboard and plastic containers and put them all together in a clear plastic bag that I hand-carry through security. I've never had any problems with officials refusing to inspect them visually.

Cancellations

In all cases, make sure that you clearly understand the charter company's refund policies in case you cancel. Nearly all companies charge a fee (often $100 or more) for cancellations for any reason before ninety days and, in many cases, will not issue any refunds with fewer than ninety days before the charter date.

Most of the larger charter companies (as well as your local travel agent) offer a travel insurance package that will reimburse your deposit after a cancellation, but you should carefully check the risks covered. In most cases, they are limited to cancellations caused by circumstances outside your control, such as medical emergencies, civil unrest, or airline strikes. Canceling a charter simply because you decided not to go is usually not grounds for a refund.

Security Deposit

All companies require a refundable security deposit to cover damage or missing gear from the yacht. The amount of this deposit varies depending upon the value of the yacht and the deductible on the insurance coverage, but it usually falls between $500 and $2,000. That deposit won't be returned to you immediately after the cruise because the company may take twenty-four hours to fully check over the boat. Paying with a credit card not only leaves you with cash for traveling, but also allows you to dispute any charges at a later date. Nevertheless, be sure that your contract specifies exactly when and how the deposit will be refunded.

Insurance

With most charters, the company provides "all risk" insurance coverage from major damage or loss of the vessel and simply includes that as part of your charter fee. Bear in mind, however, that you are responsible up to the amount of the deductible for any damage that is your fault. Be sure that you fully understand the amount of the deductible, and make sure the insurance covers the dinghy and other watercraft such as Windsurfers. Your contract will also specify the limits of liability and indemnity insurance for you and your crew, so be sure to read (and understand) all the paperwork.

Minor damage caused by the charterer, such as dropping winch handles overboard, losing an anchor, or dunking the outboard, will be deducted from the security deposit. Most charter companies offer an insurance package to cover these accidents for ten to fifteen dollars per charter day, but they do not cover gross negligence, so you must always use good seamanship and common sense.

Keep in mind also that the deductible applies to each incident and not to the entire cruise. If you gouge the hull while docking (at a cost of $500), dunk the outboard (another $500), and rip the mainsail by crew error ($2,000), you are liable for a total of $1,500 even if the deductible is only $500, because there were three separate incidents. My advice is to take the additional insurance, which then frees you from any security deposit or deductible and leaves you to enjoy your cruise without worries. You can also walk away from the boat at the end of the trip without any concerns.

The charter company will absorb the cost of any breakdowns that are not the result of negligence on your part (such as broken refrigeration) and your charter contract should clearly state that routine wear and tear is covered by the company.

Read and remember all the rules set by the charter company, since these can affect your insurance coverage. Every charter company prohibits sailing at night and, if you sustain damage to the boat while under way at night, the insurance company is likely to sue you to recover the costs. In most cases, your cruising area will be specifically outlined, so be careful to remain within the accepted limits. Before you leave, the charter company will probably ask you to sign a separate agreement stating that you understand the limitations on the charter and that you understand the rules for insurance coverage.

Read the fine print in the contract (and insurance policy) carefully, so you are aware of any exclusions. For example, most insurance policies exempt coverage for "gross negligence" or "willful carelessness," a rather broad term. When you initially book the charter, you should request a copy of the insurance policy along with the contract and, if you have any questions, consult your own attorney or clarify them with the charter company—in writing beforehand.

If you are chartering from a private party, be sure to ask for a copy of its insurance policy and read it carefully to see that it covers bareboat chartering. Few conventional marine insurance policies include chartering coverage, and this must be added with either a separate rider or a commercial charter policy. Many boat owners try to slide through on this coverage, because charter insurance is considerably more expensive than a normal policy, but such corner-cutting leaves you exposed to a lawsuit. You may have recourse against the boatowner, but you are still liable for damages or injury to a third party.

Other Problems

While bankruptcy is not a common problem in the charter business, it does happen from time to time, and more than a few charterers have lost their deposits in the process. There simply isn't any good solution to this problem, other than asking the charter company to bond your money or place it in an escrow account, which few (if any) will do because they need the money to cover operating costs. If possible, pay with a credit card such as Visa, MasterCard, or American Express, because the major card companies will refund charges made on their cards for services not received. They also act as an ombudsman when there is a dispute over charges with the charter company.

What do you do if your boat is not available when you arrive? This usually occurs only with loosely run management fleets, where the owner may suddenly break his contract with the company or the boat may be damaged beyond immediate repair. Every company has boat problems, ranging from broken masts and engines to actual sinkings, but the larger fleets usually have the resources to shuffle a number of boats as substitutes until repairs can be made.

Whatever the situation, your charter contract should clearly bind the company to provide an immediate and suitable replacement, even if it means giving you a larger yacht at the original price. No company is going to refund your travel costs or out-of-pocket expenses, which is why you should investigate travel insurance for your own protection. But at worst, the charter contract should spell out the full and immediate return of your deposit, or provide for other acceptable arrangements, such as a free charter at another time. As any lawyer will tell you, unless you have such a clause in your charter contract, you will have little recourse later.

If you have a particular reason for wanting a specific boat, such as testing it prior to buying a similar model, write to the company ahead of time and request a guarantee in writing. Also check on the policy if the boat is not ready when you arrive. Will the company provide compensation for lost time, and will it pay for your hotel room?

Inventory List

Every charter company will provide you with an inventory list of the equipment on your boat, usually covering everything from the dinghy outboard to the corkscrew in the galley. It will mention the list during the checkout and you'll probably be asked to initial a copy as well, but during the rush to get under way on your vacation, it is often forgotten.

Take the time to go over the checklist carefully before you cast off, however, because the charter company uses that same list when you return and you are responsible for any missing items. Go over the checklist item by item, and note any items that are on the list but not on the boat. As careful as they are, the charter companies nevertheless can overlook something, but this won't excuse you if you tell them when you return that the missing items were never on board.

Contract

Review your contract for the following items.

Basic Terms: dates of charter, fees, amount of deposit, schedule of payments, pick-up and return locations.

Delivery: should guarantee that the boat is fully equipped and ready at agreed place, date, and time.

Running Expenses: fuel (both engine and stove), food, drink, ice, or dockage are not included if not specified in the contract.

Redelivery: should specify in "good condition" with normal

wear and tear. Should detail any late penalties. Should draw distinction between lateness and lateness due to act of nature.

Under Way

There are two important items that you don't want to overlook while you're on your cruise: the logbook and the damage report.

The logbook is important to the charter company, because it provides necessary information about engine use, battery condition, and other operational details. Each log will vary, but generally you only have to fill it out at the end of each day with the information the company requests.

Since the logbook is usually combined with your operational checklist, it also provides you with reminders of your various mechanical duties, such as checking the engine oil and water. Even more important is the protection that a careful record of your trip can offer in case you have problems or damage the yacht later. A complete and accurate log is always a reflection of your good seamanship. Make your log entires regularly as part of the daily routine, so you won't have to play catch-up at the end of the trip.

Since you'll turn in the official logbook at check-in when you return the yacht, you might want to keep your own log as a record of your cruise. You don't need a fancy logbook and, in fact, some of the most interesting logs are simply bound blank notebooks left for the entire crew to use. These end up as memorable collections of thoughts, reactions, and notations, often illustrated with sketches or snapshots.

The damage report is just what it sounds like: a listing of the "uh-ohs" that took place on your cruise. "Damage report" sounds more ominous than it is intended to be, and you should really think of it as what pilots call a "squawk sheet." Obviously, if you drop a winch handle overboard, you should list it. But the damage report should also include everything from lights that don't work to portholes that leak. This provides a starting point for the service crew so it can correct the problem for the next charter crew. Once again, be sure to note any problems as they occur so you don't have to wrack your memory after a week of sun, wind, and piña coladas.

Check-in

It's been wonderful and you don't want to think about the realities of jobs, school, and winter snow, but the time has come to return your charter boat. Before you departed, your briefing should have covered the details of how, where, and when to return the yacht. You'll usually return to the pier of your departure, but some bases have a separate maintenance dock.

Before you reach the dock your crew should have all of its gear and clothing packed and ready for departure. You are expected to leave the boat shortly after it arrives to allow the shore crew to inspect and inventory the boat. In most cases, this is a quick process and you're soon on your way to the airport.

Your contract should specify when the company will inspect the yacht for damage, and the inspection should take place while you are present to prevent any damage that occurs after your charter from being charged to your account. A lawsuit in the Great Lakes underlined such a situation, in which the charterer left immediately to catch an airplane. Sometime later, he was billed for damage caused by a line wrapped around the propeller, which included a bent prop shaft and bearing replacements. He knew that the boat was operating properly when he returned it and, in court, it turned out that the company hadn't inspected the boat for several days, during which time it was used by some of the staff to tow other boats.

A recent charter in Tahiti illustrates how the check-in procedure can run smoothly. Using our VHF radio, we called the base one hour before our arrival as requested, and were met at some distance offshore by a staffer in a skiff, who came aboard and began to review the condition of the engine and sails as we headed toward the charter base. At this point, our crew was packing its personal gear and clothing into duffel bags, checking all the lockers for forgotten items, and happily polishing off any food left in the galley.

On the way in, we discussed the logbook and damage report with our check-in skipper and, within minutes of arriving at the dock, our crew was able to get off the boat. We settled into comfortable chairs under some palm trees and sipped icy fruit juice while the maintenance crew swarmed over the boat with inventory lists and trash bags. By the time our van was ready to leave for the airport, the check-in was complete and our deposit, on a credit card slip, had been returned and torn up. It was a painless ending to a delightful week.

POWERBOAT CHARTERS

*B*are powerboat charters are a new entry into the world of chartering, which was once confined to sailing yachts or larger-crewed motor yachts, but many areas now have yachts available for nonsailors.

Surprisingly enough, many of the powerboat charterers are actually sailors who have decided that some of the comforts of power cruising are worth giving up the pleasure of sailing for. But whether you're a sailing expert venturing into new worlds or a novice testing your powerboat skills, you'll need to be prepared for the differences in power charters.

For anyone used to sailing, powerboats have advantages and drawbacks. The first advantage is that they're ready to go at the turn of a key, unlike sailboats whose sails have to be hoisted and adjusted regularly. The second advantage is that powerboats are fast and dry. You'll be able to cruise from harbor to harbor at much higher average speeds than similarly sized sailboats and, from the protection of the flybridge, you'll miss most of the spray. In rainy weather you can retreat to the main cabin of many powerboats, where there is a second helm station for just such conditions.

The disadvantages of powerboats, particularly for sailors, are the opposites of the above advantages. The delights of a sunny afternoon under an expanse of white sail is lost on a powerboat. Even spray—that occasional mist that tingles on warm skin—is part of the sailing life-style, and not everyone is willing to give it up.

Choosing a Powerboat

In general, you get a great deal more space aboard a powerboat than you do on a similarly sized sailboat, so you need to reset your thinking when preparing to switch from sail to power. While a 45-foot sailboat may be the right size for three couples, a 40-foot powerboat may offer larger staterooms, a bigger galley, and more usable deck space for sunning.

Once again, I believe that more room for fewer people is the best choice. Just as with a sailboat, I prefer not to use the main salon for a bedroom, so that the crew isn't restricted in staying up late, getting up early, or searching for a cold soft drink at midnight. Many of the powerboats used in chartering have the ubiquitous "convertible dinette" found on sailboats, which can be converted from a dining table during the day to a berth at night. Unless you really need the extra bunk, don't count this area as a cabin. There's usually no storage space for your personal gear; you have to share a head compartment with one of the other cabins, and you have to put your bedding away by day and make your bed every evening after dinner. That's too much like work for my tastes.

This charter powerboat features an upper flying bridge with a bimini top, an after deck with permanent hardtop, and spacious accommodations for up to ten guests. (Photo courtesy VIP Charters)

When you look at a powerboat's accommodation plans, you'll probably see a few layouts with a big aft stateroom, a forward stateroom, and a smaller cabin to one side between the two.

The aft stateroom is the traditional owner's cabin on most powerboats, so it will usually have a large double or queen-sized berth, a private head compartment with shower, and such amenities as bedside bureaus, a vanity area, and a large hanging locker.

The forward cabin will also have a double berth, although it will probably be more vee-shaped to fit the bow, and it will have a smaller head compartment and less storage.

My experience has been that the smallest stateroom is the least desirable, and not just because of size. Sometimes with a double berth but more often with upper and lower bunks, it's considerably smaller and less ventilated than the others, which can be a real drawback in the tropics.

Galley Up or Down?

One choice not faced by sailboat charterers is selecting the location of the galley, which, in powerboats, can be ei-

The hinged dining table on this charter yacht folds out of the way, turning the settee into a couch for casual relaxation or conversation.

ther "up" or "down." A galley-up configuration means that the galley is on the same level as the main salon, and is usually located either to one side or in a forward corner out of the way. This layout reduces the size of the salon, but it puts the cook into the middle of the dinner hour conversation. It also provides the best view and the maximum amount of light and fresh air.

A galley-down layout puts the cooking area at the level of the forward cabins, and provides more space in the salon for entertaining. The drawback to a galley-down is that the cook is separated from the salon, either by height or by actual divider, and there is usually little or no view from the galley.

Power

Another choice faced by potential power charterers is the number of engines. Small powerboats, such as 35-foot trawlers, often have single engines, while larger yachts usually have twin

The galley-up layout on this powerboat is compact, yet has all the necessities, from microwave oven to extensive storage.

engines. Everything else being equal, twin engines have several advantages.

First, a second engine is a sizable safety factor, especially when you don't have sails to fall back upon if your single engine fails for any reason. Second, twin-engined powerboats are so much easier to maneuver, particularly in difficult docking situations or with wind and current pushing you around, that even novices can end up looking like pros. Last, twin-engined boats are generally faster than singles and, since speed is one of the advantages of a power charter, you might as well take full advantage of it. The downside to a twin-engined boat, of course, is that it consumes twice the amount of fuel, which at today's fuel prices can make a sizable difference in your budget.

Charter powerboats usually have generators, which provide an electrical supply for every possible amenity from blenders to air conditioning. Whether you care if your margaritas or daiquiris are blended may be of little importance, but an air-conditioning system can truly put you into the luxury category. If the weather is hot and humid, being able to dine and sleep in a cool environment can be literally priceless, especially if you don't have it!

But having a generator does require you to be a good neighbor. It's nice to sleep with the air conditioning on all night, but that also requires the generator to be on when you're anchored, and that creates a steady exhaust sound for the boats around you. If you plan to run your generator all night, find an anchorage away from other boats so you don't disturb the evening quiet. As an alternative, you may choose to marina-hop in your powerboat, spending each night tied to a pier with a supply of shore power for your needs.

USING THE POWERBOAT

Since they have an advantage of speed, powerboat charterers are able to leave one destination later and arrive at the next earlier than sailboats, so you can dally at anchor until late morning and then reach your next destination while the prime anchorages are still

Powerboats often moor near each other, since the noise of their generators can be irritating to sailboats without the luxury of air conditioning, microwave ovens, and blenders.

available. You can also leave early and then explore coves or islets along the way, relying on your speed to get in before dark. Whatever your choice, a powerboat widens your horizons to more distant ports, and helps you get the most out of a smaller area.

I chartered a 37-foot powerboat in Baja California several years ago, and it turned out to be one of my most enjoyable charters ever. Although it was a two-cabin layout, there were just two of us aboard, and it made a delightful yacht for a couple. The master stateroom on this sportfishing-styled yacht was forward, with a second cabin with upper and lower bunks next to it, and a shared head with shower. The second cabin was tiny and airless, and we ended up using it to store our overflow of clothes, books, and gear.

With twin engines, we had the speed to cruise far from the charter base but, instead, we chose to do a more leisurely explo-

ration and never ventured more than forty miles from home base.
But we did take pleasure in sleeping late and then watching the sailboats upanchor to set sail for their next harbor. We snorkeled the reefs or explored until after lunch, which was held in the air-conditioned salon. Even with such a late start, we were still among the first to arrive at the next anchorage, often sipping a slushy drink when the sailboats finally dropped anchor.

Powerboats also have a draft advantage, and can usually anchor in shallower water than sailboats because they don't have keels. Since shallow water is usually closer to shore, you are in more protected surroundings and will ride easier in a powerboat. Also, because most charter areas have far more sailboats than powerboats, you can usually find a good spot in shallow water even if the deeper water anchorage is crowded.

Powerboat Seamanship

Just because you have some advantages over sailboats doesn't mean you can let your guard down, however, and you need to exercise the same cautious seamanship that you would under sail.

Sailboats can usually run aground with impunity, and the worst damage is often just a little scuffed paint on the bottom of the keel. On a powerboat, however, the propellers, prop shafts, and rudders are completely exposed and quite vulnerable. If you find a stray coral head with your powerboat, you may also find that you've bent a propeller or a shaft.

Without the benefit of a keel and because of the greater windage from the larger superstructure and topsides, powerboats are more affected by the wind. When docking, you need to take the windage into account, since it can easily push you toward (or away) from a pier.

With a single engine, you'll need to be more confident in your boathandling. On your first day of the charter, practice stopping, reversing, and making tight turns just as you would with a sailboat. Most single-engined boats have right-hand turning propellers, which means the propeller turns clockwise when in forward gear and when viewed from the stern looking forward. A right-hand prop pushes the stern to starboard in forward gear, and pulls it to port when reversed. Use this knowledge to help with your boathandling. If possible, approach a dock on your port side and use reverse to both pull the stern into the dock and stop the boat.

Twin-engined powerboats don't have this pull, since the two engines rotate in opposite directions to balance each other out. With both engines in reverse, the boat will back in a straight line. But because the propellers are offset from the centerline, using either engine by itself will cause the boat to turn. For example, putting either engine alone in forward pushes the bow toward the opposite side—the starboard engine in forward will cause the boat to turn to port.

With twin engines, you'll be able to "twist" the boat within its own length by judicious use of shift and throttle. By putting one engine in forward and the other in reverse, you can turn the boat quickly to either side. Imagine that the shift levers are the rim of a steering wheel or the handlebars of a bicycle. When you push forward (forward gear) on the starboard shift and pull back (reverse gear) on the port, the boat will turn to port. Reverse the procedure, and the boat will spin to starboard.

You'll need to experiment a bit. You may require more throttle on the reversed engine to stay in position, since the propeller is less effective in reverse than when going forward.

In heavy winds, you may find it uncomfortable going directly into the swells. Choosing a course on either side of the wind and then "tacking" toward your destination will allow the boat to ride comfortably over the waves without freefalling at the top.

Going downwind in high seas is easier if you can set your speed to match that of the waves, so you aren't either catching or being caught by the swells. If possible, keep your yacht on the face of the wave so that you're always going "downhill" with maximum control and minimum effort on the engines.

CREWED CHARTERS

*I*magine starting your day on the aft deck of a luxury yacht, anchored off a pristine and deserted beach. Fluffy croissants and freshly squeezed orange juice are on the table, and sun-warmed decking is under your bare feet. This evening, you might end the day moored to the quay in St. Tropez or Antigua, watching the strollers from your yacht as you enjoy a leisurely five-course gourmet dinner in the soft evening air.

Few of life's pleasures compare with a crewed yacht charter, because it combines a superb sense of privacy with the freedom and flexibility to do exactly as you please. It's no wonder that the truly wealthy, from Liz Taylor to Donald Trump, choose yachts as their method of escape. Crewed charters have been described as "catered cruising."

"The special charm of a large yacht is that it enables presumably responsible people to combine the milder irresponsibilities of a beachcomber's existence with all the comforts of a luxury hotel," said King Edward VIII of England, later the Duke of Windsor and a man who knew his way around luxury yachts.

You can, of course, find superb service afloat on many of the best cruise ships, but you must go where they choose. Aboard a crewed charter yacht, the captain will inquire discreetly what might please you each day and, should you prefer to do nothing, you will be left undisturbed. Other options might include Jet Skis and

Windsurfers, waterskiing, sailing, snorkeling, or exploring ashore. Larger yachts have a wider selection of toys, which might include helicopters and automobiles.

Crewed charters come in two distinct varieties: the "owner-operated" crew, and the professional crew. Owner-operators are usually married couples who serve as captain and chef aboard their own yacht, which is their home as well. These yachts often operate like a cozy bed-and-breakfast inn, and you will be treated as a friend as well as a paying guest.

Professional crews are more often found on larger yachts, where they are employees of an absentee owner. They are charged with serving you in the same way you would expect at a five-star small hotel. Your wishes will be met graciously and completely, but a certain distance is maintained between the staff and the guests.

But, you say, I can't afford to charter a luxury yacht in the sixty- to two hundred-foot range. Maybe so, but first consider that

Water toys, such as this boardsailer, are available as options on most charters. In the background, a dinghy is ferrying a charter crew ashore.

a week aboard your own yacht costs no more than you would spend at a top quality resort or luxury hotel for accommodations, food, beverages, and all the other incidentals like sightseeing and those endless tips.

Although some of the largest yachts charge $100,000 a week or more, the majority of luxury charters cost far less. Ed Sacks, president of The Sacks Group, points out that three couples can have their own yacht, complete with superb food, luxurious staterooms, and an attentive crew, for around $3,000 to $5,000 a week per couple.

While most charters are designed purely for pleasure, many companies are finding that luxury yachts are ideal for truly private and relaxing business meetings away from office pressures and deadlines. Yachts are perfect for entertaining clients or hosting conferences, with stewards that cater to every need and an array of food and drink for every palate. Other companies have discovered that a yacht is the perfect business incentive, and much more of a bonus than a week at a ski resort or hotel.

WHERE TO START

Most novices are reluctant to try chartering because they don't know how to begin their quest for a yacht. Your starting point, in every case, must be with a charter broker. A travel agent is fine for booking airlines and hotels, but charter brokers specialize in matching up clients with charter yachts around the world. You might want to talk to several to find one with whom you feel comfortable. The charter broker has been described as a combination of psychologist, social counselor, and matchmaker, and the best brokers are able to ferret out the perfect boat in the perfect location for each need.

One question that you should ask each broker is, "Have you been aboard each boat and do you know the captain and crew?" Truly professional charter brokers make it a point to visit each yacht regularly, both to inspect it for condition and to acquaint themselves with the crews.

"After all," says Terry Hines of Bob Saxon Associates, "a successful charter is more about people than about a boat, so we work hard to make sure the client and crew are one hundred percent compatible."

"Although there are probably five hundred luxury charter yachts in the world," notes Ed Sacks, of The Sacks Group, "we will not put a client aboard a boat that we have not personally inspected."

In addition to knowing the boats, a good charter broker should also be familiar with the charter areas to make suggestions on possible itineraries and seasons.

The four basic questions each charter broker will ask are where, when, how many, and how much, although not necessarily in that order.

Your answers to where and when need not be ironclad unless you have a specific desire to be in one particular place and time, such as Monaco for the Grand Prix, since a broker may suggest alternatives that you may have missed. The Mediterranean high season is the summer, while the Caribbean season is the winter, but you might enjoy other areas such as the eastern United States or even as far afield as Thailand or the South Pacific. To truly enjoy a charter, seven days is the minimum required to unwind, and ten days is even better.

You do need to be honest about your budget, but don't be shy if you're not in the $100,000 a week bracket. Charter brokers have listings in all size ranges and can often match you up with more than you thought you could get.

If you're traveling with a group, Tom Collins of Tom Collins Yachts suggests that three couples are a good number, since there are many yachts with luxurious three-stateroom layouts at reasonable rates. "Besides," he notes, "larger groups have more trouble agreeing on what they want to do or where they want to go."

Because a captain and crew can make or break your charter vacation, don't be shy about asking the charter broker about them. What licenses does the captain hold? A minimum should be a 100-ton U.S. Coast Guard license, but many charter captains hold Master's papers for much larger vessels.

How long have the captain and crew been together, and how long have they been on this boat? Ideally, you want a crew that has worked together for enough time to sort out any problems and smooth out the operating routine. If the captain is new to the yacht, he may not be familiar with its full capacities yet, and he may also be less than familiar with the cruising area of the yacht. Captains and crew tend to either stay with an owner when he buys a new yacht, or stay with the yacht and move to the new owner. A crew that has worked with one owner on several yachts is likely to be above average in ability. On the other hand, a captain may have been working on a particular yacht from the start of its construction, and will stay with it through many owners because he has such a solid knowledge of it.

You should also ask (if they aren't described in the charter brochures) about the standards to which the yacht is designed and maintained. In the world of ships as well as large yachts, there are "classification societies" in the major seafaring nations that establish and administer standards for their design, construction, and maintenance. Intended to reassure insurance companies and owners that their yachts are properly maintained, a classification also assures a charterer of a seaworthy yacht.

To be classified, a yacht must have its plans approved, and a society representative inspects the yacht during construction. Afterward, the yacht is inspected regularly by the society to maintain the classification.

The most common societies in the yachting world are Lloyd's, a British society that issues the +100A1 rating; the American Bureau of Shipping (ABS) with its A1-AMS for motor yachts; and Det Norske Veritas (DNV) of Norway with the A1 rating.

SIGNING UP

Once the broker has the basic information, you'll receive a package of photographs, descriptions, and perhaps even videotapes of yachts that fit your needs.

Look at the photos and study the layouts and descriptions. If you want privacy, try to avoid adjoining cabins, because the walls (bulkheads) on yachts are not as soundproof as in houses. You'll probably see classic yachts built in the Roaring Twenties, sleek European-styled yachts with ultra-modern interiors, and sailing yachts with clouds of sail. Choose one whose looks appeal to you.

When you've narrowed your selections, the charter broker looks at the master calendar for that yacht to make sure that your dates are available.

At the time that you make the charter reservation, which actually takes the yacht off the calendar and holds your time block, you will pay 50 percent of the charter fee. You will be expected to deposit the remainder of the fee at least thirty days before the starting date. This is usually accomplished by a wire transfer so there is no delay in clearing the funds.

If you're used to staying at luxury hotels, you're probably wondering about all those "extra costs" that can increase the price. Most yacht charters are priced in one of two ways: all-inclusive, or Western Mediterranean Terms (WMT).

All-inclusive is just that: the base rate includes fuel, food, beverages, docking fees, and, of course, the captain and crew. There are a few extras, however. Although good wines and champagnes are included in the rate, don't expect to drink Dom Perignon like water. Some all-inclusive contracts specify a certain number of hours of fuel use each day, with a charge for additional running time. In addition, you'll be expected to pay for communication costs, such as long-distance phone calls or faxing.

Western Med Terms are more of an *à la carte* plan, and the base charter rate provides only the yacht and crew. Beyond that, you will be charged (at cost) for fuel, food, beverages, and incidentals such as harbor fees. Western Med Terms is popular in the Mediterranean because that region lends itself to eating ashore in the evenings, so charterers don't have to pay for unused food.

With either plan, however, you will be expected to tip the crew at the end of your cruise. This can range from 10 to 15 percent of the base fee, depending upon the yacht and the location. Tipping is usually toward the lower end of that scale in Europe and higher in the United States and Caribbean, but don't forget that this is truly a tip and should be based on the quality of service provided.

Once you've chosen the yacht and location, you'll receive a preference questionnaire from the charter broker, which will cover everything from your favorite foods and beverages to any special requirements such as computers.

LEGALITIES

You will be entering into a contract for the yacht charter, so make your plans carefully. Cancellation can cause forfeiture of your deposit as well as responsibility for the remaining fees if the yacht is not able to rebook that time period.

The ultimate responsibility for the yacht rests with the captain, and his decisions are law regarding the safety of the ship and crew. Aside from that, you are the master of the ship and can direct it to depart or dally as you wish. Each yacht is fully insured, so you need not worry about accidents.

Because of antiquated maritime laws for yachts operating from U.S. ports, you will charter under bareboat, or "demise," terms, which state that you are chartering the boat itself and hiring the crew separately. While you will probably be asked to sign a separate contract for the crew, there is essentially no difference in liability or responsibility from a crewed charter elsewhere in the world.

WHAT'S AVAILABLE?

Take your pick from a wide range of yachts. The 163-foot *Jefferson Beach,* for example, carries twelve guests in six luxurious cabins (each with shower or tub) served by a crew of twelve, for $79,000 a summer week in the Mediterranean. For those wanting speed, the 132-foot *Octopussy* is one of the fastest mega-yachts in the world at more than 50 knots, carrying ten guests in five cabins, a crew of six, plus a Jacuzzi, sauna, and nine bathrooms, for $55,000 a week based in Palm Beach. *Destiny* is a 120-foot Broward, which will be available for ten guests in New England this summer, at a rate of $45,000 a week with seven crew. At the other end of the spectrum, *Reality* is a 91-foot Broward with three staterooms and multiple water toys for $17,500 a week, while the 62-foot motoryacht *Jewell* has three staterooms and a crew of two for $9,500 a week.

COMMUNICATIONS

If you're concerned that you will be out of touch for days, rest assured. Most modern luxury yachts have better communication systems aboard than you have in your office. Aside from the standard marine electronics, charter yachts often have satellite communication systems (satcom) that allow direct dialing anywhere in the world, regardless of whether the yacht is in harbor or at sea. Telex, fax machines, and computers with modems are all available for those who want to stay in touch with business while their family plays. Many of the large yachts that regularly cater to a business clientele also have scramblers to keep your communications private.

PROTOCOL

While the yacht is technically yours, you must observe the following rules of protocol between guests and crew to have a harmonious cruise.

1. The captain is responsible for everything aboard, so you should channel all of your requests through him, unless he encourages you to do otherwise. By the same token, don't be shy about asking to help sail the boat. Most crews are happy to let you steer or trim the sails.
2. Maintain a separation from the crews, particularly on large yachts where they have more than enough work to keep them busy. In Europe, crews are seen but never heard, with private entrances to their quarters and separate dining facilities. Don't

expect them to join you on your sightseeing junkets, although they'll drop everything to ferry you to and from shore. On smaller yachts, there is more flexibility and you can invite the captain or crew to join you ashore if you desire. Don't be offended if the skipper declines, though. He may have projects to get done, or he may simply prefer to keep a slight distance from his clients.

3. Remember that the crews are not babysitters. If you bring young children, plan to care for them yourself or bring a nanny (who can often be accommodated in a smaller cabin).

4. The galley is a sacred area, which you should enter on invitation only. If you want a can of cola, ask before you start rummaging through the refrigerator. By the same token, give warning to the captain or cook if you plan to dine ashore or simply want to skip a meal—you'll save them unnecessary work with a little forethought.

On the flying bridge of a large motoryacht, charterers enjoy hors d'oeuvres at sunset, catered by one of the crew.

5. Make a point to leave the boat daily. You can go ashore, shop, swim, or explore, but give the crew a chance to clean up your cabins, prepare food, tear down the generator, or simply have a few moments of private time when they aren't "on call."
6. If you plan to invite guests aboard, that is certainly your privilege, but you should alert the captain beforehand. That way, the crew will be ready for extra demands such as stocking a bar area, having extra ice ready for drinks, or even preparing an extra helping of hors d'oeuvres.

Tipping

On yachts whose crew is hired (as opposed to owner-operator yachts), tips are often a major portion of the crew income. By custom, a normal tip ranges from 10 to 15 percent of the charter fee. This should be given to the captain, although you certainly can dictate how it should be divided among the crew, since you may want to provide monetary thanks for extra services. In general, the European tipping range is lower (10 percent), while Caribbean custom is closer to 15 percent.

What can you expect on a crewed charter? Anything you want. A typical seven-day charter along the Riviera might include stops at Monaco, Antibes, Cannes, and St. Tropez, plus exploration of offshore islands, shopping ashore, and sightseeing. In the Caribbean, you can enjoy piña coladas at lunch, water sports in the afternoon, and quiet anchorages at night.

Rikki Davis of Rikki Davis Inc. points out that too many first-time charterers try to cram in too much. "Don't try to rush around to every island and harbor. This is a relaxing vacation rather than a hectic tour. Plan to sleep late, enjoy life aboard the yacht, and make short passages when you feel like it."

Your charter broker can advise you on what clothes to take, which is usually a range of resort wear depending on your dining plans ashore. Even though these are large yachts, storage is tight, so keep hard-sided suitcases to a minimum and use folding duffel bags for most of your clothes.

What about chartering for business? The same rules generally apply, whether you want the yacht for a business meeting on one afternoon, or an incentive cruise for a fortnight. Sophisticated communications keep you in touch, but recreation is only a step away and a dive into the sea.

Whatever your preference, chartering a luxury yacht is the best way to have your fun and take it with you, too!

For more information on luxury yacht charters, contact the following brokers:

Bob Saxon Associates
1500 Cordova Road #214
Fort Lauderdale, Florida 33316
(305) 467-8876

The Sacks Group
1600 SE 17th Street #410
Fort Lauderdale, Florida 33316
(305) 764-7742

Rikki Davis Inc.
1323 SE 17th Street #209
Fort Lauderdale, Florida 33316
(305) 761-3237

Tom Collins Yachts
400 S. Hibiscus Drive
Miami Beach, Florida 33139
(305) 673-5400

Blonder Marine & Charter
1379 Main Street
East Hartford, Connecticut 06107
(203) 561-5302

CREWED CHARTER RATES

The following shows the rates for crewed charter yachts of various sizes in both sail and power.

Boat	Type	Size	Crew	Guests	Weekly Rate
Gulfstar 40	sail	40	2	4	3,850
Bahari	power	42	2	4	5,500
Swan 46	sail	46	2	4	6,450
Privilege 48 cat	sail	48	2	8	12,000
Blue Royal	sail	50	2	4	4,800
Moorings 500	sail	50	2	6	4,900
Hatteras 53	power	53	2	4	6,000
Irwin 54	sail	54	2	6	7,750
Moorings 60	sail	60	2	6	6,384
Perfection	sail	60	2	6	7,500
Windship	sail	69	2	6	8,500
Mercedes	power	98	5	6	28,000
Ladyhawke	sail	105	5	8	20,000
Bonheur 2	power	130	7	10	50,000
Endeavour	sail	130	8	8	60,000
Stefaren	power	177	14	10	175,000
The Other Woman	sail	192	12	34	154,000

WHAT TO TAKE

*O*verpacking is usually the curse of most charterers, even after dozens of trips, simply because you never know what you'll need. Indecision also enters into the equation, as does fashion, since you want to look well dressed. The result is that you carry more than you need.

There is an apocryphal and oft-told story of a man whose airline lost his duffel bag full of clothing on the way to his charter. He purchased a swimsuit, two shirts, and two pairs of shorts as interim replacements, but at the end of his charter, he found that he hadn't needed anything else!

On the other hand, in many areas you'll need to take swimsuits for sunny days as well as foul-weather jackets for rainy ones, comfortable clothing for sailing and dressy attire for shore (even in the casual Caribbean, many resorts require jackets and ties for men and dresses for women).

Carrying Your Clothes

Soft luggage is essential, at least on board the boat, since it has to stow easily into oddly shaped nooks and crannies. While many sailors routinely ship their duffel bags on airlines, I prefer either to stuff mine into a hard-sided suitcase or repack when I get to the charter base, moving the contents of the suitcase into a duffel bag that was also inside. The empty suitcase is then left with the charter company, which has provisions for such storage.

Duffel bags come in all sizes, shapes, and materials. If possible, get ones with padded handles for easier carrying, as well as a detachable shoulder strap to tote them through airports. I own half a dozen big duffels, but my favorite is made of Acrilan (which is used for boat covers) and is thirty inches long by twelve inches in diameter. Admittedly I don't travel light, but this seabag has plenty of room to spare. The only other noteworthy features are a pair of zippered pockets on the outside for gear I want to keep handy. I've had duffels with inner liners, dividers, and even side pouches for dirty laundry, but the simple cylindrical duffel seems to offer the most flexibility in packing.

Whether they are rectangular or cylindrical doesn't matter, but don't pick a seabag too small. To support the load, the handles should be part of straps that extend all the way around the duffel, and the zipper should be plastic or other nonrusting material. Be sure the zippered opening extends from one end to the other for maximum access. The duffels in my closet are made from canvas, Acrilan, Dacron, and even Kevlar, but I haven't found that one is superior to the others. One source for good duffels and other soft luggage is Land's End (Dodgeville, Wisconsin 53595).

Packing and Unpacking

Some sailors like to live out of their seabags, and pack them so they resemble tidy drawers. Others immediately unload their duffels into the drawers and lockers in their cabin. Either way, store your clothing in a dry location. Check drawers for watermarks. As insurance, you may want to line the bottoms with plastic trash bags. With today's shallow-hulled yachts, the bilges aren't always deep enough to contain the bilgewater, which can slop up into lockers.

If you're carrying dress shirts, pants, blazers, or dresses for shoreside use, you may want to invest in a soft suit carrier that can be hand-carried aboard an airplane and stored intact in a hanging locker aboard the yacht.

Everything else in your duffel bag should be tightly rolled. This not only takes up the least amount of space, but also keeps the wrinkles out of sweaters and pants.

What to Wear

What you wear is obviously going to be a function of where you're going and in what season. Fall cruising in New England (or England, for that matter) is going to be vastly different from French Polynesia.

Regardless of your chartering area, you can plan on getting wet from an occasional rain shower or simply from spray. Take a water-repellent lightweight jacket or windbreaker, or a light foul-weather jacket. If you expect the rain to be more than infrequent, consider taking foul-weather pants and seaboots. For an early summer charter on Loch Ness in Scotland, I wore full foul-weather gear daily and was thankful I had it.

Even if you're sailing in a warm climate, don't forget the wind-chill factor, which can make the most sweltering day turn nippy offshore. For each knot of wind, the temperature lowers by one degree. For example, the Tradewinds in the South Pacific regularly blow at twenty knots. With an air temperature of 85°F, you'll be feeling just 65°F of temperature. With the boat sailing into the wind, the apparent wind might drop that wind-chill temperature to 55°F.

At the opposite end of the spectrum, you need to consider both heat and sun. Sunburn protection consists of long-sleeved shirts, long pants, and hats. Cotton fabrics breathe best in the tropics, and you can find loose-fitting shirts that will keep you cool as well as protected. Light colors are the best for reflecting heat.

Carry a pair of socks and underwear for every day, plus spares depending upon how likely it is you may get wet. I also carry spare athletic socks to prevent blisters from poorly fitting swim fins.

Layering is the modern approach to staying warm and dry, and modern fabrics now wick dampness away from the skin. Under a lightweight outer shell of windproof water-resistant fabric, you will find piles or buntings that are soft and comfortable in all conditions. By adding a soft shirt or sweater underneath, you have layers that can be added or removed as your body is warmed or cooled.

Take two swimsuits, so one can be drying while the other is being worn, and don't forget loose T-shirts for sun protection while swimming. I also take a pair of worn-out sneakers to wear as foot protection while wading or swimming around reefs.

Be aware of local customs as you pack, because many popular charter areas remain quite conservative in their beliefs. Women going ashore in bikinis are often frowned upon, and men without shirts are equally offensive.

Other Items to Take

On page 231 is a checklist of items you may wish to take on your charter for comfort, safety, or amusement, including the following gear.

While every charter company offers masks, snorkels, and swim fins, either as part of the yacht gear or as options, serious snorkelers usually bring their own equipment to assure a comfortable fit. If you wear glasses, you may want to invest in a prescription mask.

A camera is essential to record your cruise for posterity, and be sure to bring plenty of film. By the time you add up the cost of airfares, charter, and food, a few extra rolls of film is a pittance compared to the increased pleasure the photos will bring when you return home. The basic camera kit should be a 35 mm camera fitted with interchangeable lenses. I prefer to use a couple of different zooms, such as a 28–85 mm lens for on-deck candids, and an 85–210 mm lens for capturing more distant scenes. Use a clear filter (such as a skylight or UV) to protect the lens from scratches and spray. You'll also want a polarizing filter that can eliminate reflection and add dramatic tones to the sea and sky. A flash is useful for shooting inside the boat or in the evening.

Masks and snorkels are available at most charter bases, but serious charterers often bring their own to assure a good fit.

With today's modern electronic cameras, it's wise to carry a spare battery, which may be of a type that you can't find in your charter area.

Polarized sunglasses with leather patches on the sides protect the eyes from stray light and can be vital for piloting in shallow water, since they allow you to see the various colors of the water (and hence the depth) more clearly.

A canvas tote bag is easy to pack, and you can use it for a multitude of tasks. I've used mine to carry blocks of ice back to the boat, to carry sweaters and a camera ashore, and to bring back the booty purchased in local shops. Even on uninhabited islands, you can use the tote to bring back the inevitable shells, rocks, or other items that don't fit into pockets.

Every charter boat is equipped with flashlights, but they're often bulky and heavy. A small pocket flashlight slips into a jacket pocket for everything from guidance while walking on dark piers to reading menus in candlelit restaurants. It should be small enough to hold in your teeth, leaving both hands free to struggle with a shackle or an outboard motor. But remember the joke that a flashlight is just a tube used for storing dead batteries: always add new batteries before your trip.

Fun and Games

This is a vacation, so don't be shy about taking a selection of toys for your own amusement. I always carry a stack of paperback mysteries or spy novels, which also make great gifts or barter with the locals.

It is surprising that while every charter yacht has a good stereo system (some even have cassette disc players), the selection of tapes is uniformly abysmal. If you enjoy Beethoven, you'll find only heavy metal and vice versa. Take your own tapes with you, and also keep an eye open for tapes of local music during your shopping trips. Some are awful, but many are good and will be fun to hear again at home.

If you're like most charterers, you'll be curious about the world around you, so take a few compact guidebooks to add some background to your cruise. A guide to tropical shells, for example, can open up new vistas in your reef explorations, and a book on birds can solve the ever-present "what was that?" question.

By the same token, a foreign dictionary or phrase book can go a long way toward cementing relationships with the locals, and help you find the nearest bakery, liquor store, or bathroom.

Two packs of playing cards are a starting point for ferocious evening games of Hearts or Canasta in the cockpit. You may also want to bring along some of the travel-sized boards for Scrabble or Monopoly.

It's helpful to have a small plastic sewing kit on board when you've lost a button or a seam is starting to let go.

You can never have too many plastic bags with Ziploc seals. Take several different sizes, and use them to carry shells, extra or exposed film, spices, bandages, dirty laundry, wet swimsuits, your papers and money when going ashore in the dinghy, and a thousand other things.

If you are a yacht-club member, you may wish to include your club burgee to fly from your yacht. I've done this several times, and it's always surprising to have someone row across to say they know someone in my club, or even to have club members arrive unexpectedly in the same anchorage. A tradition for yacht clubs worldwide is to trade burgees, so I generally carry a couple extra, and I've returned with the flags of yacht clubs from Ireland to Monaco.

To make sailing easier, carry a pair of sailing gloves that have the fingertips cut off so you can still tighten shackles. Reinforced palms provide protection against rope burns. I also carry (in the ubiquitous plastic bag) a pair of old garden or work gloves. These are perfect to keep the slime and tar off my hands when anchoring, as well as for protection against sharp barnacles or coral fragments. A rigging knife is equally important, since it has not only a sharp blade for cutting, but also a marlinespike for loosening knots and a tool for opening shackles. Keep it in your pocket when you're sailing.

This isn't exactly chartering gear, but I always bring several disposable ear plugs, purchased in pilot shops near airports, to block out screaming children or jet whine on the flights to and from the charter. In addition, I carry a soft eyemask to block out the light and allow sleeping in daylight during long flights (as well as on the charter boat when I want to sleep late).

Seasickness remedies, in prescription, ear patches, or over-the-counter pill form, are important even if you're sure you won't be ill. You might want to include Kaopectate or Lomotil prescription pills to combat the spicy foods or uncertain water found in some areas. Sting kits are available in most drug stores, and they can ease the pain and itching from mosquito bites, bee stings, and other encounters with local bugs. If you are taking prescription medication, carry an extra supply. An extra pair of prescription glasses can replace the ones last seen descending into deep water after you leaned over the rail.

For cold-weather chartering, add a watch cap to keep your head warm, and gloves to do the same for your fingers. I like wool turtleneck sweaters under my foul-weather jackets, both for the warmth and for the antichafe protection around my neck. You might also want to include a terry-cloth towel to wrap around your throat and keep any drips from penetrating inside your jacket.

Some charterers carry their own toilet paper, as many parts of the world use something about the consistency of sandpaper. Just be sure it is fully biodegradable and suitable for holding tanks. Several small bars of neatly packaged hotel soap can be used if the local soap is unacceptable for any reason.

As far as paper and plastic money, I always take my passport. Even if it's not needed for the charter, it simplifies identification in any situation. Traveler's checks are the best and safest way to carry money, and are redeemable nearly everywhere. Credit cards are also widely accepted—often, even a remote shack on a nearly deserted island is equipped with a credit card imprinter.

THE SKILLS

SEAMANSHIP

*T*his chapter isn't intended to replace any of the standard books on seamanship and boathandling, but it reviews certain skills that you'll need to manage a bareboat charter.

First of all, be willing to accept advice. If the charter company warns you against a particular harbor, don't go there. If it tells you not to go out in twenty-five-knot winds, don't do it. And don't, unless it's a dire emergency, ever sail at night.

Second, there must be one person in charge at any given time. Since you'll be sailing with other people, you may want to rotate those duties daily but, at any moment, only one person should be making the decisions and issuing the orders. If you aren't comfortable sharing the ultimate responsibility for the yacht, you should make that clear before the charter is booked. Otherwise, you might find yourself in a situation where a life depends upon the correct actions, and any shouting match can only prove dangerous.

The first rule of seamanship is preparation, so you should make sure the boat is ready for use. Check the engine daily for oil and coolant as well as belt tension, and also check the fuel level. After starting the engine, keep an eye on the gauges for oil pressure, water temperature, and charging rate to see that they are normal. Poke your head over the stern to make sure cooling water is coming out of the exhaust.

In addition, you should plan to check the bilges daily for any leaks. You'll probably find some water dripping from the prop shaft, so pump the bilge dry daily to see if an abnormal amount of water is entering the hull. Since freshwater is so precious, check the tanks daily and compare the amount used to the number of days left. If there seems to be a shortage, make sure the crew is aware it needs to conserve fresh water.

Some rules of seamanship are basic, but bear repeating. Because chartering is a vacation sport, be careful about alcoholic consumption. It doesn't take too many piña coladas in the midday sun to cause a serious deterioration of your response time and reasoning ability. If necessary, select a "DH" (designated helmsman) to run the boat without imbibing. Better yet, wait until you are anchored for the night before you open the bar.

The Checkout

Your first test of seamanship is going to be a tough one, since the charter company will want you to demonstrate your abilities with a spin around the harbor. With the experience of watching hundreds of different skippers, it can quickly assess your ability and your confidence in boathandling. Your run-through might feel similar to approaching a pier in front of a crowd of spectators—just thinking about the possibilities of error can make you nervous.

On the other hand, however, checkout skippers aren't looking for perfect boathandling, particularly on a boat that is unfamiliar to you at this point. What they want to see is a level of common sense. This might include your decision, even while being watched, to make a second pass at a pier when you think the first try isn't going to work out. It might be your resistance to being rushed through a quick checkout or your insistence on asking questions about everything.

Every checkout skipper is different, but they've all read your sailing résumé and know your background. They may ask you to back away from the dock, pick up and then drop a mooring in midharbor, and return to the dock, or they may have you take them for a short sail under your command. As the editor of a national yachting magazine, I was on and off hundreds of boats every year in the course of my writing duties, but I didn't get special treatment at charter bases and neither will you. Sometimes they simply handed me the keys and helped with my docklines, but more often I was put through the full battery of tests.

Start by briefing your crew on what you expect them to do. By delegating responsibilities clearly, you enable everything to take place with a minimum of difficulty and confusion. One person can handle the dinghy to keep the towline clear of the propeller, another can be responsible for tending the fenders if you're moored alongside a pier, and others will handle the bow and stern lines.

You should also alert the crew to what you *don't* want done. For example, if you've planned your approach to a pier perfectly, one crewmember jumping prematurely from the bow with a dockline can push the boat away from the pier and ruin your approach. You'll need to let them know which lines, bow or stern, should be cleated first, where to put the fenders, and what to do with the dinghy.

Be wary of pierside spectators, too, since they may know nothing about boats. More than a few yachts have crunched into piers when a line was tossed to someone on shore who then helpfully pulled hard on it, which threw off the entire approach.

On your checkout as well as during the cruise, take everything slowly and don't try to show off.

Private Testing

I have a first-day practice of going through a series of sea trials to "learn" the boat. Once clear of the dock, I stop the boat and back it down at various speeds to see how well it responds to the rudder and power settings. Because of the propeller rotation, most sailboats tend to pull to port when backing up, so take this into account when planning your approaches and departures. If you need to back a sizable distance, one solution is to use power to get the boat moving steadily, and then put the engine in neutral. In this way, you can steer the boat easily in either direction, since the prop is no longer exerting any pull.

I also check the turning radius by spinning the boat hard-over in each direction. You'll find that, for the same reasons of propeller thrust, you'll turn tighter in one direction than the other, which may be of use to you in an awkward situation.

To judge the way, or inertial speed of the boat, I find a buoy or similar marker in calm water. From a slow speed, see how much reverse power is needed to stop the boat right next to the buoy. This will give you an idea of how much power is needed when docking or anchoring.

By spending a little time to learn the traits of your charter yacht, you'll be much more comfortable during the cruise as you face anchoring, docking, or other maneuvering situations.

Leaving the Dock

Until a boat is moving, there is no steering control, which makes leaving a dock more difficult than coming into one. If at all possible, try to power away from a dock going forward, since sailboats are not at their best in reverse, and you need as much control as possible.

It may seem foolish, but before you start any maneuver, you should count the docklines. A great many skippers, including famous racing sailors, have found themselves embarrassed to discover that someone forgot to release one last dockline and no amount of engine power was going to move the boat.

When leaving, you can simplify your crew's work by "doubling" the mooring lines. In other words, run the line from the boat around the cleat or piling and back to the boat, so it can be released from on board. This eliminates the last-minute clambering back aboard that can be awkward.

Decide on your course of action before releasing the docklines. To get the bow of the boat away from the dock, one of your crew can either push it out or, alternatively, pull in the stern to lever the bow away from the pier. The latter is probably the best course, since it keeps anyone from falling into the water. Be sure to use fenders to protect the hull from scraping the pier.

Spring lines can help you get away from a pier, especially if

On this Moorings 500, all the lines lead to the cockpit for ease of use.

you're boxed in by neighboring boats. By reversing against a doubled aft spring line (with other docklines released), the bow will swing out into open water and you can then release the spring and go your merry way. Use a doubled forward spring line and power forward to swing the stern away from the pier. Either way, have someone stand by with a fender for hull protection.

Docking

Rule one for docking a charter yacht is to use the engine and have the sails down and furled. Rule two is to approach as slowly as possible, but with steerageway to control the boat. Brief the crew on where you expect to stop the boat and which docklines should be secured first. You might want to outline the procedure if you miss on the first approach, so that you don't wind up with one crew on the dock securing a dockline while the boat is trying to circle around for a second try.

Approach at a shallow angle, turning the bow out to swing

the stern in, and using reverse to stop the boat as the bow and stern lines are passed ashore, or crewmembers step ashore. Note that I said "step," because the boat should be close enough to safely step onto the pier or float. Too far out and your crew may wind up in the water if it misjudges or slips while jumping.

Moorings

Moorings are easy to pick up and leave, particularly when compared to either docking or anchoring, which is why mooring buoys are popular in many chartering areas.

Leaving a mooring is as simple as releasing the mooring line from your bow cleat, dropping it overboard, and signaling the helmsman to back away.

Just as with anchoring, you should be under full power to pick up the mooring. If you're not familiar with the mooring, you might want to circle it once to get a good look at it. In most cases, there will be a ring on the top of the buoy with a mooring line attached, which you'll want to pick up using your boathook. If there isn't a line, you'll need to use one of your own, doubling it to return to your boat for release.

Approach the mooring buoy upwind and moving slowly. Your foredeck crew should point at the buoy, since it will probably be out of sight from the cockpit as you get close and, when the buoy is within reach, the crew should signal to stop with a clenched fist. In some parts of the world, mooring buoys also have stern anchors attached: after securing the bow mooring line, you pull up a stern line that is then secured at your stern to hold the boat from swinging.

Only when the mooring lines are secure can you leave the helm and shut down the engine, and there have been some calamities when the crew relaxed before the boat was moored.

Heavy Weather

It may seem obvious, but the simplest way to prevent problems from heavy weather is simply not to go out in it. Charterers, who have limited time and a preplanned itinerary, however, often set sail in conditions that would make them think twice in their harbors at home. If the wind is blowing steadily over twenty-five knots, you're in for a wild ride and perhaps injury or damage unless you are competent and well prepared. By the same token, it's not surprising that the competent and well-prepared crews are usually the ones who decide to spend another day at anchor rather than venture out into rough seas and marginal conditions.

If you're already at sea when bad weather is approaching, be prepared to shorten sail early. Waiting until your boat is overpowered just makes the job of reefing the mainsail and furling the jib even more difficult. Any time your boat is heeling more than 25°, you're probably overpowered and sailing inefficiently.

In the tropics, you can see squalls approaching from a great distance, with a tall pillar of black rain slanting upward to the clouds. Before the rain is even close, the wind can quickly build from fifteen knots to well over thirty knots, so the wise skipper reefs the mainsail long before the squall arrives.

In preparation for heavy weather, be sure that all hatches and ports are closed and gear belowdecks is stored safely away so it won't fall on someone. Wearing a life jacket is a wise precaution, especially if you expect to be on deck for reefing and other work. A second towline on the dinghy is a good idea and you should probably remove any oars or other gear that might blow out or float away.

Depending upon the severity (and expected duration) of the squall, you may choose to depower the sails before resorting to a reef. The mainsail should be flattened with the mainsheet to remove the draft, and you can ease the traveler down to leeward to put a big bubble in the luff of the sail. The jib can also be depowered either by easing the sheet and allowing a similar bubble to form in the luff, or by rolling it up and reducing the sail area.

If you expect the weather to be unpredictable, by all means practice putting in reefs in light airs. You may discover a missing line and, at worst, you'll know exactly how to reef when you need it.

Most charter yachts have a "jiffy" or "slab" reefing system with a line through an eye on the leach and another line (or a hook) for

In most tropical charter areas, a squall is easily visible long before it arrives, allowing a prudent crew time to reduce sail or prepare for the increased winds.

the luff, and it's a good idea to keep both lines in place even in good weather.

Your first step is to tighten the topping lift to hold the boom up, and then ease the mainsheet. Lower the halyard enough so that the reefing line on the leach can be tightened to pull the sail snugly to the boom. At the same time, pull down the reef line on the luff (or put the grommet over the hook) and then rehoist and tighten the sail with the halyard. Ease the topping lift, trim the mainsail back in, and you'll find the boat a much changed (and much more comfortable) yacht.

Knots

Everyone aboard should understand how to tie five basic knots: the square knot, the clove hitch, the double half-hitch, the bowline, and the figure-eight.

A square knot, which is two overhand knots together, is used to tie two lines of the same diameter together. The most common use aboard charter yachts is a version of the square knot called the reef knot, where you leave a bow sticking out so it can be untied by simply pulling the bow out.

A clove hitch, two loops atop one another, is used to attach docklines to pilings or to tie fenders to lifelines.

A double half-hitch is an adjustable knot that slides, and is also used on pilings as a dockline.

The bowline is a reliable knot for making a nonslipping loop, and is used to attach jib sheets to the sails, as well as lines to other fittings. A bowline rarely jams, and is a good all-purpose knot.

The figure-eight is also called a stopper knot, since it is tied in the end of sheets to keep them from running out through the blocks. Tie it a few inches in from the end of the line so it has room for slippage, and use it in place of the overhand knot, which is hard to untie.

ANCHORING

*W*ithout a doubt, anchoring is the most common problem for charter crews. Unfamiliar waters (and bottoms), unfamiliar boats, and unfamiliar anchors all lead to dragging anchor and fouling other people's anchor rodes. Simply trying to find a suitable location with enough room in the general harbor congestion can contribute to high blood pressure for the skipper and crew.

The key is planning ahead in every aspect of the anchoring procedure. Where do you want to lie? How much scope and swing do you need? Where are the anchors of the other boats?

As a charterer, you've probably anchored before, but let's go over some of the basics so you don't miss anything.

Again, you must make perfectly clear at the beginning of your charter that one person, and only one person, is in charge. You may choose to change captains each day, but the captain at this moment is the only one to issue orders.

Unless engine problems prevent it, you should always anchor under power since you'll have more control and fewer distractions around you. Some charter boats have two different types of anchors (a CQR and a Danforth, for example) and you should ask your charter company when and where to use each anchor for best holding.

Preparing to Anchor

First, clear the decks for action. Stow the sunpads that clutter up the cockpit and foredeck, put away the soft-drink cans and bags of potato chips, and coil down any halyards or lines that might get in the way.

One person on the foredeck should be responsible for handling the anchor, and it's often beneficial to have the same crewmembers handle the anchoring every day—this makes for an experienced team. At this point, the crew should unlash the anchor. If the anchor rode is a combination of chain and line, bring enough rode up on deck to be sure that it hasn't tangled from bouncing around during the day's sail. Chain is less likely to tangle, but you might want to bring a little up just as a precaution, since tangles are likely to occur on top rather than in the middle or bottom.

Speaking of tangled anchor rodes, your crew should know how to reach a snarl through the locker door in the forward cabin. As a safety precaution, the rest of the crew should do nothing to the anchor while this is going on.

As you enter the harbor, shorten up on the dinghy painter so that it won't wrap around the prop as you back down. If you have a large enough crew, assign someone to keep the dinghy under control during the anchoring procedure.

The sails should also be furled securely, so they won't come loose at a critical point and block your vision or create steering problems. You should be prepared for any emergencies, including engine failure, snarled anchor rode, or crew overboard. If things are not going as planned, the best decision is to make a second pass after regrouping. Pressing on usually only makes a bad situation worse.

During one charter to Catalina Island aboard a Cal-46, I approached a mooring buoy and put the engine in reverse, but nothing happened. We had enough speed to get past the neighboring boats and, once into open water, I scrambled into the engine room to see what was wrong. I found that the prop shaft was turning, and the transmission was shifting properly. Returning on deck, I overheard one of our crew comment on how clear the water

102 THE SKILLS

(Above) Off the coast of French Polynesia, this charter crew is able to see the bottom clearly, which allows them to check on their anchor regularly.

(Below) For novices, picking up a mooring is the simplest and safest way to overnight. This yacht, at Catalina Island in California, is securely attached to a permanent mooring buoy.

was—and that you could see a shiny three-bladed propeller on the bottom! Sure enough, it was ours. The prop nut hadn't been properly secured and, when I shifted into reverse, the propeller had spun itself right off the shaft. That's not a common occurrence, of course, but it underlines the need to be prepared for any contingency.

Since it's often difficult to hear commands over the wind and engine, work out a set of hand signals between the foredeck and helmsman. These should be one-handed, since the foredeck crew may be holding the anchor rode (or simply holding on) with the other. In general, a closed fist means stop, a pointed finger means turn in that direction, a lowered palm or thumb means back up, and a raised palm or thumb means go forward. There's nothing more amusing than watching a crew anchor in a flurry of shouted commands and frayed tempers, and a simple signaling procedure can make you look like a pro even on your first charter.

Power slowly around until you find a suitable spot that has sheltered water, good bottom for holding, enough depth even at low tide, and enough room to swing without interfering with other boats. Always approach the point where you drop the anchor from downwind (or down current if the current is stronger than the wind) at idle speed.

Stop the boat above where you want the anchor to rest and, when your forward motion is gone, signal the crew to lower the anchor enough to hit bottom. When it hits bottom, the crew can signal you to back down as it eases out the rode. When suitable scope is out, snub the anchor and check to see if it is holding.

Once you're settled in, it's not a bad idea to "swim the anchor." As part of your afternoon snorkeling, pull yourself down the anchor rode and see if the anchor is really set solidly. As a final precaution, take anchor bearings on shore objects so you can quickly check to see if your position has changed. If possible, pick objects such as lighted signs that will be visible at night.

Anchor Etiquette

In anchoring, the first boat in has priority. That means the first boat decides whether to use bow and stern anchors, or whether everyone swings on a single anchor. The first boat also has first choice of location.

As later skippers arrive after you, tell them where your anchor is located so they can stay clear, and insist politely that they anchor at a safe distance. You may encounter resistance and, if you're concerned, simply move to another location. You'll sleep better at night.

Dragging

If another boat drags anchor, wake up your crew and prepare to start the engine, but don't do it until absolutely necessary. Even then, use a flashlight to make sure that you won't tangle your propeller in someone else's anchor rode. If you can, simply fend off the other boat using fenders, but be very careful that you and your crew do not get your hands or feet between the boats. If there is a swell, watch out for rigging problems if the masts roll together.

Make note of the yacht name, type, and identification number as a precaution, even if you don't think any damage was done. You may find damage in daylight that you missed at night.

Last, be kind to the other skipper, because he's bound to be scared and upset. Everyone drags sooner or later, and someday it may be you in this situation.

If it is your yacht that drags, get one or more competent crew up and start the engine immediately but leave it in neutral, since you may need power quickly.

Check the anchor rode to make sure that it hasn't broken or chafed through. If you aren't in immediate danger of hitting other boats or going aground, see if you can let out more scope to reset the anchor. Aside from feeling the anchor rode to check the tension, a boat with dragging anchor will pitch up and down, and the bow will hunt from side to side as the anchor skips along the bottom.

Evaluate the weather as you consider your options, since it may have been a wind shift that caused you to drag. If that occurred, is your anchorage still protected or should you find a safer harbor?

Once the yacht is safely anchored, the cockpit becomes its social center, but don't relax until you're sure the anchor is holding. (Photo courtesy of The Moorings)

If you still can't get the anchor to stick, it's time to start over. Raise the anchor to water level and have your foredeck crew inspect it to see if it is fouled with muck or grass, or if it appears to be bent.

At night, be sure to switch on the depth sounder and look at the chart so you don't go aground while reanchoring. Try to find another spot with a sandy or mud bottom that will provide good holding. Once reanchored, take bearings on shore objects for position checks later. If the weather is turning unstable or you have concerns about the anchor holding, you may want to stay up for an hour or so as a precaution.

At dawn (4:00 A.M.)during one Scottish charter with my parents, our placid mooring turned into a raging lee shore as a sudden storm approached, and we were literally pitched out of our berths and forced to set sail for open water rather than risk staying so close to danger. If you find yourself in the same situation, check the charts and simply find an area where you can sail around until dawn brings the opportunity to find a safer refuge. Don't try for another harbor or cove, unless you're absolutely certain of both your seamanship and your navigational skills.

Raising Anchor

Once again, assign someone to tend to the dinghy and power slowly ahead, taking hand signals from the foredeck crew to keep the bow following the anchor rode as it is winched aboard. Don't use the anchor windlass to pull the boat forward, but simply to take in the slack—let the boat engine do the work.

If the anchor doesn't break free of the bottom, check to see if you're fouled on someone else's anchor. With clear water, you may be able to see that you're snagged on a coral head, and you can unwrap with directions from your crew. As a last alternative, use the stern anchor to temporarily reanchor while you dive down to find a solution to the problem.

Med Mooring

Probably the biggest difference between cruising in Europe (and in some Pacific islands as well) and cruising in North America is the so-called "Med moor," in which the yacht is backed into the quay, secured by a bow anchor and stern lines ashore. An alternate method is to moor bow to the quay.

Because European harbors are so small (and often overcrowded), this method allows all yachts to lie parallel to one another, separated by fenders, and taking up the minimum amount of precious quay space.

You might want to practice this before your charter (or during the checkout period with a charter company adviser aboard), but you'll get the hang of it quickly.

As with all anchoring procedures, the key is to brief the crew fully beforehand, proceed slowly, and remain calm. In addition, Med mooring requires that you use lots of fenders, including at least one on the stern. You'll need to have a good anchor and

Identical Swan yachts moored Med-style at the dock in St. Martin.

substantial chain, because European harbors are notorious for being deep but having poor holding.

As you enter the harbor, your first task is to choose the mooring spot. Use binoculars to select a space with convenient cleats, bitts, or rings, and check to see if there are reasons the space is empty, such as a sunken boat (I've seen this), a rock, or a protruding drain pipe from the shore.

The ideal location is lying parallel to the wind, so your boat isn't being pushed one way or another. Those spots fill up quickly (and early) in most harbors, so if you're arriving after midday, you can expect to find the premium moorings taken. Since many quays nearly encircle European harbors, you'll also need to decide between an upwind and a downwind mooring.

Everything else being equal (such as the distance to town or the proximity to a smelly fishing fleet), I prefer to moor with the wind pushing the boat off the quay. That makes the holding of your anchor less important, and it provides a natural buffer that keeps your stern from tapping expensively into the quay.

If you're lucky enough to find a slot with the wind parallel to your mooring, simply round up and drop your anchor, then back into the available space. Most sailboats have rather poor directional control in reverse and often pull one way or the other (find this out during your checkout). If your stern starts to sag off to one side, your anchor handler can add a little tension to the anchor rode to straighten the bow out.

If, however, the wind is off the beam, you'll need to drop your anchor at an angle to windward to hold your bow from being blown down on the leeward boats. Try not to anchor over the rodes of the other boats if at all possible, but know that it may be the only possible way. You can always straighten out things once you're secured and, in any case, you're likely to be the first to leave in the morning anyway.

With the wind abeam, your foredeck crew can maintain a light strain on the anchor rode to help hold the boat in position, although you may have to go forward and back in a crabbing motion to fit into your slot.

As you near the quay, snub the anchor and back down hard. With any luck, the anchor will dig in and you will stop short of the quay. If the anchor does not bite, you'll need to power forward and start over with more scope. Once dug in, you can release some rode to get the stern close for a crewmember to step ashore with the stern lines (or you can pass them to one of the bystanders waiting for you to make a mistake). If you have crosswinds, be sure to pass the windward stern line first.

In most European ports, you'll be securing to a bollard or a ring. In either case you should dead-end the stern line at your cleat and pass it around (or through) the bollard/cleat and then back on board. That will make it easier for you to adjust for tidal changes without going ashore, and your departure will be simplified if you can slip the stern line as you power away.

If the bollards or rings are widely spaced, they will keep the stern centered properly in your mooring slot. If not, you should cross your stern lines so they act as spring lines to keep you centered.

Mooring bow to the quay is growing increasingly popular,

especially as more sailing yachts have long reversed transoms that quays love to bite. As a result, many charter yachts have walk-through pulpits that make going ashore easy. Mooring bow-in is easier, since you can maneuver the boat better in forward than reverse, although you'll have to drop the anchor off the stern as you approach your spot. You'll need to rig a bridle to center the anchor line astern if you don't have a cleat in midtransom. Otherwise, your boat won't lie parallel with the other boats. Mooring bow-in also gives you better privacy from the evening strollers on the quay, who otherwise can look directly into your open cabin, although some sailors enjoy sitting in the cockpit in the evening and watching the passing parade.

Mooring bow-to is also easier if you're shorthanded, since the skipper can pay out the stern anchor rode with one hand while steering with the other. Once close to the quay, cleat off the stern anchor and leave the engine idling in forward while you walk forward to handle docklines. If the wind is across the mooring, just leave the helm turned slightly to windward to hold the boat up while you go forward.

When going ashore, move the boat away from the quay for safety by taking up some rode and easing the stern lines. If you have a gangway, fold it up for safety in case there is surge. A word of warning: Many European harbors have regular ferry service, and these powerful ships can generate a surge that will bounce you around like a toy in a bathtub. Be prepared to move away from the quay when they enter the harbor, and leave your boat far enough away for safety when you go ashore or tuck in for the night.

When departing, you may be lucky enough to slip your stern lines, power forward over the anchor, and raise it neatly. On the other hand, you may also bring up one or two other anchor lines that have crossed yours. Good seamanship and common courtesy suggest that you should alert the other yachts to reset their anchors and haul in the slack on their anchor rode.

A few last tips on Med mooring: Don't forget to hang a fender over the stern (or over the bow) as well as over each side when mooring to keep the quay at a distance. If you think the harbor bottom is cluttered with debris or mooring chains, attach a buoyed trip line to your anchor to help with your departure (as well as to mark it for late-arriving boats). Don't be afraid to warp the boat in if there are strong crosswinds or current, using the dinghy to run the stern line ashore after you've set your anchor.

Bahamas Mooring

Another anchoring style unfamiliar to most North American sailors is the Bahamian moor, which uses two anchors to allow a boat to swing in a small diameter. Popular in the Bahamas from which it gets its name, Bahamas mooring is also used in areas of strong and variable current such as tidal streams or estuaries worldwide.

In essence, you will set two anchors 180° apart and position the boat midway between the two. But instead of leading the anchor rodes to the bow and stern as usual, lead both lines to the bow, so that the boat will pivot freely in all directions.

Most Bahamas mooring takes place in fairly shallow waters, so you'll have enough rode on each anchor to either drop back or power forward to set the second anchor. This allows you the choice of first dropping the stern anchor as you enter the mooring area and then powering forward to set the bow hook, or setting the bow anchor first and then dropping back to set the stern. The choice depends upon your own preference and the abilities of your crew. If you don't have enough anchor rode to set both hooks, you can simply tie the two rodes together in the middle and then power back to the midpoint after each anchor is set.

If possible, try not to set your anchors parallel to the current, so that your boat will stay on one side of the anchor rodes. This will eliminate the corkscrew twist caused when the boat circles the two mooring lines all night. At worst, you'll need to untwist the rodes by hand before you depart.

If you need more scope to handle a temporary increase in wind, you can ease the scope on one anchor rode as though you were riding to a single anchor. When the weather stabilizes, reposition yourself at the midpoint to keep your swinging circle at a minimum.

NAVIGATION

$\mathcal{F}$or the most part, navigation in the chartering areas is easier than finding your way around a large city. If you have any qualms about your navigational abilities, courses from the U.S. Power Squadrons or U.S. Coast Guard Auxiliary can sharpen up rusty skills or add new ones.

Most of the popular charter areas are suitable for sailors with rudimentary navigational skills. The ability to plot a compass course, keep track of position, and read a chart are the most frequently required skills. In the Virgin Islands, for example, you are always within sight of land, although you may lose that contact occasionally during rain squalls. In Scandinavia, on the other hand, there are so many islands (and they are so similar) that you need to pay close attention to the chart to keep track of where you are in the maze.

Navigation in the Caribbean consists of watching for underwater hazards on the charts when cruising close to the islands, and plotting compass courses to make passages between the islands if the visibility is low.

For many sailors, part of the fun of chartering is the preplanning that goes into deciding the itinerary, and this starts at home. You'll want a current guidebook for the area, and you can order these from one of the many nautical bookstores such as The Armchair Sailor (543 Thames Street, Newport, Rhode Island 02840,

(800) 292-4278). From reviewing this guidebook, you'll be able to decide on harbors or anchorages to visit during your charter. Don't wait until you arrive at your charter yacht to start thinking about where you want to explore.

As you work out your plan of action, compile a list of questions to ask at the briefing. These might cover anything from the location of the best anchorages or snorkeling reefs to the procedures for entering a foreign port. You'll want to make full use of the local knowledge available during the briefing to check on sights, restaurants, hazards, and weather conditions.

While doing your preliminary planning, you'll be selecting the places you want to visit and planning your route, but be sure to consider several factors:

1. The length of the charter
2. Prevailing winds
3. Crew ability
4. Tides and currents
5. The distance between harbors.

Novice charterers often try to cover too much territory in too little time. A charter is intended to be relaxing, so rushing from one harbor to another can turn a vacation into a frenzy. Some experienced crews prebudget one day as a spare, which they can spend at any time during the cruise when they find a place they want to linger or an unexpected area to explore. In many areas of the Caribbean, you may be sailing less than twenty miles a day, with time available for leisurely lunch stops or afternoon swims, before reaching your anchorage for the night. Trying to cover one hundred miles a day is simply pushing too hard.

The prevailing winds will shape your cruise, since you'll want to pick courses that are as easy to sail as possible. You'll probably find a few beats to windward in most areas, and scheduling those early in the cruise allows you to drift home in an easy manner.

The crew's ability is important when choosing the area of your charter, and comes into play again as you select courses. If you have novices aboard, don't set your sights on long beats to windward in the open sea, or you'll have a discouraged crew. Instead, try to break up any difficult sailing with stops along the way. Seasickness is equally important to take into consideration. In the Abacos, for example, you can sail for miles inside the reefs and islands in perfectly flat water but if you venture outside, the seas can be steep and challenging.

Currents are a function of the tidal variation. In the Caribbean and Mediterranean, the fluctuation is minimal so currents are generally weak. In the British Isles, Northern Europe, and Scandinavia, planning your cruise around the tidal almanac can be crucial to reaching your destinations.

Distance between harbors is usually short in most cruising areas, but you'll want to keep safe refuges in mind in case the weather changes suddenly on you. This isn't as crucial in the Caribbean, where distances tend to be on the shorter side, but European cruising can expose you to longer spans between harbors.

Once you arrive at your charter base, you'll get the precharter briefing. A company representative will walk you through your cruising area, using the charts found on your yacht. You should be prepared to take notes, because you'll literally be covering a lot of ground in this session.

Common Sense

Since every charter company absolutely forbids any nighttime navigation, you'll have to contend only with daylight hours. Be realistic about daylight, too, because it can be scary (and dangerous) if you misjudge when the sun sets. In many charter areas, beacons and other aids to navigation are rather casual, and sometimes do not operate at all.

When the sun sets, it's often like turning out the light. Don't count on the lingering dusk of urban areas, which comes from the atmospheric pollution that glows for an hour or more after sunset. Darkness comes quickly in clean air.

If the sun is setting and you aren't sure you have enough time to reach another harbor, you don't. Stay where you are and leave the next morning instead of putting your boat and crew in danger. Also keep in mind that if you have an accident while sailing at night, your insurance is invalid and you have full financial responsibility for the yacht.

Eyeball Navigation

In some areas, the water is so shallow that you have to consciously relax and not panic when the depth sounder reads just a few feet under your keel. In fact, I once sailed for more than a week through the Bahamas with less than four feet on the sounder during most of the cruise.

Water color is the key to eyeball navigation. The paler the water, the shallower it is. Using your chart (which you should always keep handy in the cockpit), you'll get a feel for the patterns of shallows and reefs in the area you're visiting.

If you're concerned about a tricky passage, the best conditions for eyeball navigation are a sunny day with the sun high and just behind you. Conversely, the worst time is in overcast weather, or with the sun ahead of you causing sparkle on the water. In fact, many experienced skippers simply won't attempt a difficult entrance in those conditions.

Polaroid sunglasses should be a part of your charter kit, since these lenses both intensify the color and eliminate surface glitter. With Polaroid lenses, you get an almost chartlike definition of the deeps and shallows around your boat.

Sand reflects white in shallow areas or very pale blue in slightly deeper areas, while grass and rocks show up as dark blotches where you won't want to anchor. Coral heads are a yellowish color. As you tiptoe through shallow waters, you'll quickly acquire a knack for eyeball navigation, and it's nothing to be feared.

Navigational Tools

For the Caribbean, the depth sounder is an essential part of your navigational toolbox, and you should ask at the briefing where the transducer is located. If it is near the bottom of the keel, you will know that whatever reads on the sounder is your clearance from the bottom. If, as on most yachts, the transducer is located in the hull itself, you'll need to add in the depth of the keel to find out how much water you have beneath you.

Also for the Caribbean, a hand-bearing compass can be useful for plotting position by using various points on the islands. A set of parallel rules will give you compass courses, and dividers will give you distances.

For European chartering, the previous items are essential, along with either a radio direction finder or a Loran, which is usually called a Decca in Europe. With good radio beacons and Loran signals, you can use either to provide good position fixes when you're out of sight of land. Some newer yachts also have Global Positioning System receivers that lock on to satellites to give you a location accuracy of a few hundred feet.

Charts are essential to your cruise, and these should include overall views of the cruising area as well as detailed charts of the important harbors or anchorages. Most charter yachts will have at least one guidebook, and there may be a homemade guide from a charter company as well that duplicates your briefing.

"Placemat navigation" is a standing Caribbean joke, since many restaurants use plastic-coated charts as place settings, and more than a few sailors have navigated by using these miniature renditions of local harbors and anchorages. Don't put too much faith in them, however, because they're usually long out of date.

If you want to bring your own charts and guidebooks as I often do, contact The Armchair Sailor bookstore for one of its fourteen free lists of necessary charts and technical publications for various cruising areas worldwide. Just tell the shop where you're going, and it can provide the list as well as the items on it.

I generally take my own 7 × 50 binoculars, since I usually find that the ones provided aboard the yacht are corroded from long hours left in the cockpit.

Aids to Navigation

Be sure that you know which system of buoys is used to mark the waters in which you are sailing. There are two types of buoyage systems in use worldwide: lateral and cardinal. The lateral system marks the direction to a danger relative to the course that you should follow.

The cardinal system, however, indicates the direction of a danger relative to the buoy, and cardinal refers to the cardinal points of the compass.

In 1985, the International Association of Lighthouse Authorities (IALA) designated two systems of buoyage: System B (combined cardinal and lateral), which the United States uses, and System A. IALA-B, with red buoys kept to the right when returning to harbor (red-right-returning) is now in use in both North and South America, Japan, Korea, and the Philippines. IALA-A, where red buoys mark the port side of the channel, is used in Europe, the British Isles, Scandinavia, Australia, New Zealand, Africa, and in some parts of the Caribbean and Asia.

Communications

The VHF radio is your lifeline in most charter areas, and Channel 16 is used for distress and calling other yachts, but you should switch promptly to a nonpriority channel for other conversation. In areas such as the Caribbean, most of the charter companies use a particular channel for their communications and, if you have problems or questions, they monitor that channel during the hours their base is open. Find out at the briefing about their channel and hours of use.

DINGHIES

A good dinghy is as critical to a successful charter as food and water, but the dinghy can also be a recalcitrant child that you have to watch all the time.

Chartering around the world, you'll encounter a wide variety of dinghies and soon will become a connoisseur of the good and bad in small boats. In Europe, inflatable dinghies are popular because they are used for going to and from piers or quays, and their soft sides are easier on the hull of the charter boat. In the Caribbean and tropics, where dinghies often must be dragged over coral reefs and onto beaches, rigid dinghies are the rule. In many areas, the older wood or fiberglass dinghies are being replaced by hard-bottomed inflatables, which combine the strengths of both types. This is a slow process, however, since hard-bottomed inflatables are expensive and charter companies are adding them only as others go out of service. Request a hard-bottomed inflatable if you can, since they are more stable, tow better, and are quieter when bumping against the hull at night.

Dinghy Checkout

Too many charter skippers concentrate on learning about their yacht and overlook the dinghy, only to find later that the oars don't fit or the outboard won't start.

During the checkout procedure, be sure that the oars fit into

In Europe, inflatable dinghies such as this Avon are popular because they protect the hull of the charter yacht from scratches and gouges.

the oarlocks, and that they not only are the proper size for the dinghy, but also are the same length. One-piece oars are essential, because the two-piece styles tend to be flimsy and frustrating. With your checkout instructor present, start the outboard yourself to make sure that you understand any quirks it may have. Every dinghy should have a long painter for towing, a bailer, and a light anchor with enough rode to use on a reef.

The outboard should have a spare shear pin if it uses it, since you might bump the propeller on a coral head. The outboard should also be secured to the transom with a safety line in addition to the usual screw clamps.

If you have an inflatable, be sure you understand how to add air to keep it firm, and see that the charter company has left an air pump for that purpose.

Dinghy Seamanship

When boarding a dinghy, always step into the middle and sit down as quickly as you can to prevent a capsize. Never—ever—step on the gunwale unless you're planning to go swimming. Don't stand up in a dinghy either, even if you heard that George Washington did it on the Delaware.

You'll quickly learn the comfortable capacity of your dinghy, and you should be careful not to overload it, especially if the sea is choppy. You should also carry enough life vests for everyone in the dinghy.

Before casting off from shore or your boat, make sure the engine starts and is running smoothly, or you may find yourself rowing back against wind and current. Always carry the oars with you in the dinghy, for just those reasons. If you plan to use the dinghy after dark, always carry a powerful flashlight, both for spotting obstructions and for signaling if you have a problem.

If the engine on your charter boat fails, you can use your dinghy for power. Tie the dinghy amidships with both bow and stern lines, and use fenders to protect the hull. With someone in the dinghy to control the outboard throttle, use the rudder of the charter boat to steer. You can counteract some of the tendency to turn away from the dinghy side by aiming the outboard in the opposite direction.

Before you leave in the dinghy to explore, tell the crew where you're going and how long you'll be gone. This is not just common courtesy to keep it from being stranded on the boat, but also a safety precaution in case you don't return on time.

Beaching

Most good anchorages have calm water, so running the dinghy ashore is simple. Watch for rocks and coral heads as you approach shallow water. Aim for the spot you want with enough speed so that when you reach shallow water you can shut the engine off and coast ashore until the boat bumps the bottom. Step out and pull the dinghy up. If you can't coast far enough, use the oars to pole yourself to shore.

Every beach has areas where the waves are smaller than elsewhere. Scan the beach for these spots as you approach. Beaching a dinghy in breaking waves can be a hair-raising experience.

In a perfect world, you would time the approaching swells and land between waves, quickly stepping out to drag or carry the dinghy ashore. I wish it always went that smoothly.

Since it doesn't, be prepared to get wet. Carry cameras or other valuables in plastic bags that are securely sealed. If you do capsize on a wave, keep an eye on the dinghy so it doesn't injure you.

Once ashore, pull the dinghy above the high-water line, even if you only plan to stay for an hour. It's too easy to lose track of time and return to find the dinghy gone. If possible, tie the painter to a tree or rock, or use the anchor for added security.

Docks are simple compared to beaching, but be sure to leave enough length in the painter to handle the change in tide. Many charters have returned from a day ashore to find their dinghy dangling from the pier by the painter in areas of higher tides. Secure the oars inside the dinghy with rope, and don't leave any valuables behind.

It's an unfortunate part of life in the Caribbean that many areas have so-called "boat boys," who are highly trained extortionists. When you go ashore, they offer to watch your dinghy for you, with the implied threat that it may be gone if you don't give them a few EC dollars. It's a good idea to accept this blackmail, if only for peace of mind.

Towing the Dinghy

Many dinghies are lost while being towed. It's always back there bobbing along behind you until someone suddenly says, "Hey, where's the dinghy?" and it's gone.

Part of the problem is that many charter companies use the yellow polypropylene braided line for the painter because it floats and is less likely to be wrapped around the propeller while maneuvering. But polypropylene line is both slippery and stiff, so it doesn't secure well to a cleat. I've watched as one of these painters slowly released itself, an inch at a time, from a cleat in spite of having two hitches on top.

This dinghy is securely tied astern by a single line, but with a squall looming up, it would be wise to add a second towline.

There are several solutions: One is to knot the end of the polypropylene line so it can't slip past that point, and another is to secure the cleated line by knotting it back onto itself. The third, and my favorite, is to use a spare dockline as a second towline for security. That way you're protected if the primary line slips or breaks, and you have an extra strong towline in case the dinghy capsizes.

Before towing, remove any extra gear from the dinghy, including the outboard motor, which usually stores on a bracket on the stern pulpit. When removing the outboard, be sure you have safety line secured to the big boat since this is a prime opportunity to drop the motor overboard accidentally.

If your dinghy swamps or capsizes while being towed, don't try to continue. A filled dinghy is a dead weight and can break the towline or tear out the towing eye easily. If you can't bail out the dinghy, try pulling it up on deck using fenders to protect the hull, or rig the mainsheet on the boom as a hoist to get the water out of the dinghy before proceeding.

The Outboard

Outboards on charter yachts seem to come in two types: flawless and frustrating. Flawless outboards start with a single pull, run forever on one tank of fuel, and are light enough to lift easily to and from the dinghy. Frustrating outboards require a mystical chant to start on the twentieth pull, spew smoke and fumes, and weigh a ton.

Feeding the outboard properly is one way to keep it happy, and you should use the right fuel (usually eighty-five octane) and the correct fuel-to-oil mixture (usually 50 to 1). Check with the charter company for details, or ask it to supply an extra five-gallon can of outboard fuel with the boat.

If you dunk the outboard, either through capsizing or by dropping the engine, rinse it immediately with fresh water and then rinse it with gasoline several times. Try to start it promptly and, if it fires, run it until it is dry. Whatever you do, be sure to tell the charter company it was dunked so it can take appropriate action and not pass it on to an unsuspecting charterer.

To prevent accidental dunkings, check the screw clamps on the outboard for tightness each time you use the dinghy, since they can vibrate loose.

Storing the Dinghy

Where should you put the dinghy at night? If there's a light breeze, just tie it to the stern and it will float behind you all night. But if the wind dies, dinghies just love to come up to the charter yacht and tap gently on the hull next to your bunk until they get attention.

In calm conditions, you can tie the dinghy alongside with fenders, but if the wind or the sea comes up, it will thump enough to keep you awake. On larger boats (or with smaller dinghies), you can tie the dinghy to the anchor line, where it will swing around the anchor line without hitting the bow. Another alternative is to attach your spinnaker pole to a chainplate, aiming it outboard with the dinghy at the outer end, where it will circle harmlessly all night long. The drawback is that rigging up the spinnaker pole every night creates a tangle of lines, but you'll sleep soundly.

SAFETY AND FIRST AID

*S*afety should be foremost in every skipper's mind, and a well-prepared crew always has a plan of action ready for every situation, whether it's a crewmember falling overboard, an engine failing during anchoring, or a flash fire in the galley. In general, emergencies occur with less frequency aboard charter boats than aboard the average private yacht, simply because charterers are more alert and haven't been lulled into complacency by familiar surroundings.

During the checkout, pay particular attention to the location of fire extinguishers (including Halon systems for the engine), life jackets, and shutoffs for stove and engine fuel. Your crew should also know how to use the VHF radio (and what channels are monitored in your area), as well as the location of flares and other signaling devices.

Simple housekeeping can also prevent accidents, and you should coil all sheets and halyards neatly and promptly. It's easy to leave vacation gear such as books, jackets, and swim fins lying on deck, where they can cause accidents. Tidy up regularly.

Managing Safety Hazards

Crew Overboard

When chartering in warm water the dangers from hypothermia are minimal, but an exhausted swimmer can be in serious trouble, so immediate action is always required. In general, nonswimmers should wear life jackets when outside the safety of the cockpit. Particularly in the tropics, nonswimmers might want to bring their own life vest. Called a Flotation Aid, these can be found in styles that are comfortable to wear, unlike the bulky "Mae West" jackets that discourage use.

The five steps to a rescue effort are as follows:

1. Stop the boat
2. Get buoyancy to the victim
3. Get the boat alongside safely
4. Connect the victim to the boat
5. Get the victim aboard.

Traditional methods of rescue have proven to take too long, and the current thinking is the so-called "quick-stop."

As soon as someone falls overboard, the helmsman must assign someone to watch and point at the victim. Even in smooth seas, a person's head can be very difficult to spot.

The helmsman should then immediately tack the boat. This may seem dangerous to the sails or mast, but modern rigs are tremendously strong, and the first priority is to stay near the victim. If you are running wing-and-wing downwind, you need to let the jib sheet run free through the end of the pole and, if you are using a spinnaker, you simply head up while releasing the spinnaker halyard. The sail will come down fast into the water, where you can retrieve it wet but easily.

Once stopped, you need to provide buoyancy to support the victim. The fastest way is to throw a life cushion, and every charter boat should have one within easy reach of the helmsman, perhaps even in use as a backrest. Throw it slightly upwind so it will drift down toward the victim.

As you return, you need to plan to slow the boat alongside the victim so you can throw him a line. During this process, shout encouragement to the victim, which can prevent panic on his part. Stopping the boat next to the victim can be tricky. You may want to head into the wind and stop next to him, or you can heave to by tacking without releasing the jib, which will allow the boat to move slowly at about one knot.

A line with a large loop can be thrown to the victim to keep him from drifting away and to pull him alongside the boat. Once the victim is alongside, the biggest difficulty will be getting him back aboard. Most charter yachts have swim platforms on the stern with ladders but, in any sea, these can be dangerous because of the up-and-down movement of the yacht. A ladder rigged amidships is best, or if you have enough crew, you can simply muscle the person back aboard.

If you have the opportunity, you might want to practice a man-overboard drill on your first afternoon sail using a life jacket or a cushion as a "victim."

Keeping your crew aboard is just as important, and they should always wear nonslip sailing shoes when on deck, if only as protection against the many toe-stubbers found on sailboats. Remember the old adage "one hand for yourself and one for the boat" when working around the deck. Even if you're just lolling in the bow pulpit enjoying the spray, always hold on.

FIRE

The galley is the most likely place to have a fire, either from grease or a flash-up from cooking. All of your crew should know where the fire extinguishers are located, as well as how to remove them from their brackets and trigger them.

Shout "fire" to alert the entire crew, and grab the nearest fire extinguisher. Spray it at the base of the flames.

If the fire involves liquefied cooking gas such as propane,

shut off the fuel supply immediately and let it burn itself out. You may want to keep nearby wood or fabric doused with water to prevent the fire from spreading.

Gasoline, grease, or diesel fuel fires must be extinguished with Type B fire extinguishers. Don't ever use water, which will only spread the flames. Electrical fires should be fought with Type C extinguishers, although once the electricity is shut off, what usually remains is a simple wood or fabric fire.

In the event of a fire, have a crew member gather additional fire extinguishers from elsewhere on the boat and, if they aren't enough, send someone to borrow extinguishers from nearby boats.

If you are offshore and the fire isn't extinguished immediately, send a distress call giving your boat's description, location, and the nature of your emergency. If you are able to put the fire out, use the radio to cancel the distress call. If the fire burns out of control, you will have started a rescue effort.

Running Aground

As with all emergencies, don't panic. Running aground is something that all sailors do at one point or another, and usually more often than that. In the Bahamas, it's so common that it's called "bump-and-go."

If you're under sail, you should promptly lower the mainsail and furl the jib to keep from going further aground. Don't worry about being tidy—just release the halyard and get the wind out of the sail. If you're under power, quickly put the engine in neutral and shut the engine off to keep from sucking debris and sand into the cooling system.

If the weather is reasonably calm and you've simply strayed a bit out of the channel, you have time to sort things out. If, on the other hand, the wind or seas are pushing you onto a reef or lee shore, there's no time to waste.

First, look for deep water. It will obviously be back along your path, but there also may be deep water nearby that is closer or easier to reach.

If there is no bottom debris in the water, start the engine and try to back the boat off the shoal. Heeling the boat by putting the entire crew on one side can help, and you can swing the boom out to leeward and let the crew sit on it to give leverage for heeling.

If heeling doesn't work, shut the engine down again to prevent overheating, and break out either the bow or stern anchor to kedge yourself off. Put the anchor in the dinghy and then row it out into an area of deep water. Carry only the anchor in the dinghy, and have someone pay out the remainder of the rode as you row away. Try to find a spot in line with either the bow or stern so that you'll have a straight pull, rather than trying to turn the boat as well as pull it free.

Once the anchor is set, use the anchor windlass to take up the slack and combine the pull with the engine to get free. If the anchor windlass is not up to the task (most aren't), use a jib sheet winch on the anchor rode and crank yourself off by hand. If you have an all-chain rode, you'll need to fasten a sturdy dockline to the chain, and then lead the line to the winch.

If all else fails, set both anchors to hold the boat from drifting further into danger, and call the charter company for help. You may be approached in the meantime by other yachts or by locals offering to help, but be wary. Salvage laws are very complex, and you should agree on a price before any work is begun, or you may encounter legal problems later.

Flooding

If you discover that water is entering the boat, your first action should be to activate all the electric bilge pumps manually (don't rely on float switches, which can jam open). Some of the crew can gather manual pumps or buckets, while the rest start a search for the location of the leak.

Unless you've run aground or had a collision, the most obvious places to look are the thru-hull fittings for the head, sinks, or engine. Nine out of ten leaks are caused by a hose either breaking or pulling off the fitting, allowing seawater to gush in at a substantial rate. Close the seacock to stem the flow, and then reattach the hose using double clamps.

If the seacocks and hoses are sound, you should check the stuffing box for the propeller shaft, the exhaust system for the engine, and any other openings in the hull such as a speedometer sensor.

One charter boat crew that suddenly found its floorboards underwater searched frantically for the source of the leak, and it wasn't until a crewmember happened to taste the water that it discovered one of the freshwater tanks had emptied itself into the bilge.

If you find that a hole is causing the leak, heel the boat as far in the opposite direction as you can to keep the hole close to the surface, where the pressure of the water is less.

Use torn-up curtains, sheets, pillows or anything you can find to stuff into the hole, holding it in place by wedging something against it (a floorboard or an oar, for example) from inside. This should stem the flow enough to allow the bilge pumps and your buckets to keep up, and you can make way slowly to the nearest port for emergency repairs.

If you find yourself losing ground against the incoming water, and either can't find the leak or are unable to stop the flow, it's time to send out a distress call. As before, give description, location, and an estimate of how long you can stay afloat.

As a last-ditch effort, close the freshwater seacock for the diesel engine and remove the intake hose from the seacock, putting it in the bilge. A diesel engine sucks an incredible amount of water through the cooling system, and as long as you can keep the intake clear of debris, it may allow you to stay ahead of the water.

Collision

The first rule when a collision is imminent is to make sure your crew doesn't attempt anything heroic. Keep your feet and your hands away from any point of contact, because the idea of simply pushing apart a pair of multi-ton yachts is absurd.

Your first task after impact is to check the safety of your crew and that of the other boat. A hard collision may have thrown people into the water, and they must be rescued before anything else is done.

Once assured that everyone is safe, assess the extent of damage. Has the hull been punctured? If so, is it above the waterline or below, where you may be taking water?

The collision may have broken your shrouds or damaged the chainplates that support the rigging. If so, rig halyards to help support the mast.

If possible, either hail or radio the other yacht to get the name of the owner and his address for insurance purposes. At worst, get the name, homeport, and description of the yacht.

As soon as possible, radio the charter company and report the incident. It may want to send a boat to assist you, or it may attempt to track down the other party involved. Once you've squared everything away, you should write a detailed report for insurance purposes. Shock and time can serve to make your memory fuzzy, so get this done as soon as possible.

Wrapped Propeller

Everything is going perfectly and then, suddenly, the dinghy painter disappears under the stern at an amazing rate and the engine suddenly dies. The line is wrapped around the prop, a waterborne version of having your shoelaces tied together.

When you first realize that the propeller is eating rope, shift into neutral immediately. This will minimize the possibility of damage to the bearings or shaft.

It's sometimes possible to simply unwrap the prop by judicious use of tension on the line while the engine is shifted briefly into the opposite of the gear it was in when the line was wrapped.

If this doesn't work, it's time to get out the knife and go for a swim. Don't attempt to cut the propeller free until you're in smooth water, because the combination of a boat rolling and pitching in swells and a knife can be a dangerous combination. Once you've found calm water, a good swimmer should go overboard wearing a safety line tended by someone on deck. A serrated kitchen knife seems to work better than most rigging knives, but anything sharp (including a hacksaw) will do the job. Simply carve away the line, being careful not to cut yourself in the process.

Once cleared, restart the engine and gently put it in gear. If you feel a rumbling or vibration, the prop shaft may be bent. Check the stuffing box to make sure that you aren't taking any water, and call the charter company for its recommendations. Even with a bent prop shaft, you'll probably be able to motor enough to anchor, although long distance powering is probably not a good idea.

Mechanical Failure

The two most common failures aboard a charter yacht are the refrigeration and the engine, and most can be traced to operator negligence.

If your refrigerator is suddenly not keeping things cold, perhaps you haven't run the engine enough to allow the compressor to work. If there is an on-off switch for the refrigeration, perhaps someone has accidentally turned it off. Aside from these simple remedies, your best solution is to call the charter company for advice.

Engine trouble is more likely to be a result of operator error. Any charter company has endless stories about charterers who forgot to turn the ignition on at the electrical panel, or who left the master switch in the off position. Diesel engines are relatively foolproof, so make sure that it isn't operator error before calling the charter company.

To keep from embarrassing yourself, check the simple things first, such as ignition switches and master battery switches. Make sure that the shift lever is in neutral, since most engines will not start in gear.

If the engine cranks over but doesn't catch, check the fuel flow. Is the fuel shutoff open and is there actually fuel in the tank itself? Bad fuel isn't an uncommon problem, so take a look at the fuel filter to see if it is clogged.

If the engine doesn't crank at all, are the batteries dead? Tapping the starter gently with a hammer may free it if it has gotten stuck.

If the engine was running and suddenly stopped, check the temperature gauge. If the engine is overheated, it may have a clogged water intake that caused the engine to expand and seize up. Clearing the water flow and allowing the engine to cool down may solve the problem, but be sure to alert the charter company so it can check for any long-term ill effects to the engine.

General Rules

Anyone left aboard while the rest of the crew goes ashore must have the engine keys and should know how to operate the boat. At worst, you should devise some sort of recall or alarm system to get the crew back from the beach if the anchor drags or something goes wrong. This can be as simple as raising the flag upside down, or as planned as bringing a pair of hand-held radios from home for just that use.

A basic rule on charter boats is that there is no swimming without someone else watching, preferably on deck. The buddy system is a proven method for staying out of trouble, and you should always snorkel in pairs and stay together.

If you're anchored in an area with current, it's a good idea to trail a line behind the boat with a life ring or floating cushion attached to it. Swimming against current is a good way to exhaust yourself, especially in warm water. A line astern can be used to pull in someone who either falls overboard or becomes exhausted swimming in current.

Warm water can be inviting, but don't stay in too long, especially if you don't swim regularly at home.

First Aid

With any luck, you won't even open the first-aid kit during your entire charter (except during the checkout, when you make sure it is fully stocked, of course).

Many regular charter sailors carry a Red Cross first-aid manual, or one of the many books aimed at nautical first aid, to augment whatever they may find aboard the yacht. Several such books are listed in the Bibliography.

As a minimum precaution, several of your crew should have

basic Red Cross training, covering the Heimlich technique to clear an obstructed airway, external heart massage, and cardiopulmonary resuscitation (CPR). Training courses usually include the basics of treating broken bones, bleeding, burns, and shock.

Preparing yourself mentally is just as important as having a complete inventory of medical supplies. Before leaving home for your charter, the entire crew should complete a medical survey that outlines any history of medical problems, with particular attention paid to chronic illnesses such as heart disease, asthma, diabetes, hypertension, or epilepsy. Crew members should list any prescription medications they take regularly and, if a crewmember is on medication, he should consult his doctor regarding the impact of sudden withdrawal. If anyone has allergies to medicines, foods, chemicals, or insect bites, these should also be noted. In case of a medical emergency, such information can prove vital for immediate diagnosis and treatment by a physician unfamiliar with the patient.

Sunburn

The biggest medical problem faced by most charter crews usually is sunburn, which can be avoided with some simple precautions. Many charter areas are warm and in the tropics, where the sun is directly overhead for much of the day. Bring an ample supply of sun protection, and make sure you wear it during the daylight hours, particularly from 11:00 A.M. to 2:00 P.M. when the sun is at its peak.

Modern sun protection comes in a variety of creams and liquids marked with a Sun Protection Factor (SPF). The higher the number, the longer it will protect you from burning. Sure, you want to go home with a tan to show off to your friends, but a sunburn can be painful and medically dangerous.

One way some people prepare themselves for chartering in the tropics is to go to a suntanning salon before they fly to their destination. A good base tan can go a long way toward protecting you during those early days of the charter.

Be particularly careful on overcast and hazy days, which can lull you into complacency. Don't count on the bimini top or awning for complete protection, because the sun reflects well off the water and can produce painful burns even in the shade. Don't be fooled by cool breezes, which only mask the intensity of the sun in the tropics. Wearing a hat (with a safety line in case it blows off) and a loose shirt is your best protection.

Be careful while swimming and snorkeling, since water is no protection from the sun and an hour or two floating facedown over a reef can turn you as red as the proverbial lobster. Wear a T-shirt while snorkeling for protection.

Noses, lips, and ears are particularly vulnerable to sunburn and, while there are numerous products specifically to protect those areas, the best remains white zinc oxide. Not only is it inexpensive and effective, but you can always tell when you need another layer.

Many suntan creams advertise that they are waterproof or stay on while swimming, but believe those claims with caution. The exertion of swimming can cause your body to sweat even though you don't notice it, which helps rinse away the protective layer. After swimming, add more sun protection.

Last, be careful about certain medications that can increase your reaction to sunlight. Ask your doctor if any of your prescription drugs create light sensitivity, and see if you can take a substitute for the duration of the charter.

Seasickness

Another common malady, seasickness is simply uncomfortable for most people, but can be incapacitating to others. In any case, it can ruin the day or even the trip.

People who are prone to motion sickness should prepare themselves with medications.

In general, over-the-counter antiseasickness pills have unpleasant side effects such as drowsiness and dry mouth. Prescription medications are more effective, and many sailors have switched to scopolamine, a drug released through the skin from a patch worn behind the ear. Unlike pills, it is not lost if the wearer does become sick. Another remedy gaining in popularity is a wrist band that places a small plastic dot on an acupuncture point to prevent motion sickness. Whether it is a pill or a patch, any seasickness remedy needs to enter your system as early as possible (usually eight hours for pills, four hours for patches) to give your body a chance to build up resistance before you test it offshore.

Even experienced offshore sailors get queasy, so seasickness is nothing to hide. Be careful of your diet and stay away from greasy foods, questionable foreign foods, and too much alcohol.

If you do start to feel queasy, stay on deck and focus on the horizon to help stabilize your inner ear. A distraction, like helping to steer the boat, can also prove beneficial. If you are ill, use the leeward side of the boat (or a bucket) and be sure to hang on firmly. Nourish your body with fluids (no alcohol) and rest, and you'll soon be back on your feet.

Bites and Stings

Jellyfish, bees, and wasps are common in the typical chartering areas, so be prepared to deal with bites and stings. For jellyfish, Portuguese man-of-war, or other stinging fish, do not use the commonly touted remedies of ammonia, alcohol, baking soda, or meat tenderizer, all of which stimulate a discharge of the nematocyst, or stinging cell at the end of a tentacle. Instead, neutralize the toxins with vinegar or the commercial product Stingose. Antihistamines such as Benadryl and pain medication such as Tylenol or Demerol can reduce the pain and symptoms. Apply hot towels to the affected area. If the pain persists or side effects develop, see a doctor promptly.

Bee, wasp, and hornet stings are marked by a small red area with swelling, itching, and heat. If there is a stinger present, remove it gently and then apply ice to the area. Watch for a severe reaction, which is marked by breathing difficulty, nausea, weakness, and difficulty in swallowing. If you have crewmembers with a special sensitivity to insect bites, have them carry one of the sting kits available by prescription.

Medical Emergencies

The "ABCD rule" is the basic formula for urgent medical crisis, and when injury occurs, you should survey the situation with these in mind.

"A" is for airway as well as control of the spine. Anytime there is a serious injury above the clavicle, you should assume there is a neck fracture. Clear the airway without tilting the victim's head by gently pulling the jaw out and down, and use a finger to keep the tongue from blocking the airway.

"B" is for breathing. If breathing has stopped, one person should begin CPR techniques immediately while others continue to check for injuries. In addition to checking whether the victim is breathing, be sure to observe the effectiveness of breathing, since chest injuries and rib fractures can impair the breathing process.

"C" is for circulation. Check the pulse immediately for frequency and strength. When you press on a fingernail, the color should return within three seconds if circulation is adequate. If there is external blood loss, control it with pressure on the wound.

"D" is for disability. Is the victim conscious and responsive? With head injuries, check the pupils to see if they react to light. Note whether the pupils are small or large, and whether the eyes move in all directions. Last, examine the entire body for broken bones or other trauma that may have been overlooked previously.

As you are surveying the victim, have a crew member send a "Mayday" call on Channel 16 of your VHF radio, requesting immediate radio assistance by a doctor. By radio, a doctor can decide whether emergency services such as the Coast Guard should be brought into action, or whether the patient can be treated on board your boat.

PROVISIONING AND COOKING

You'll have a variety of options when it comes to provisioning your charter, ranging from a do-it-yourself effort at a local market near the charter base to a yacht completely provisioned from a list provided by the charter company. There are, of course, many variations in between, and most experienced charterers rely on such a combination.

After you've contracted for the charter, you'll receive an information package that will include a list of food and drink with prices. You'll also be provided a list of equipment found on the yacht, and you'll need to have both lists available as you plan your menus. You don't want to order the ingredients for a particular meal and find that you don't have the utensils to prepare that food.

Full provisioning requires the least amount of effort as well as the highest cost. By checking off the desired items on the charter-company food list, you eliminate any need for shopping when you get to the charter base, and the food is usually already waiting on board your boat in cardboard boxes for you to stow away. This is simple, but you're also paying premium prices for your ingredients.

Partial provisioning allows you to select certain items from the checklist, and then augment it either before you set sail or in various ports during your charter. In this way, you can have the charter company supply bulky or heavy items (such as cases of soft drinks or juices) so you don't have to tote them around an unfamiliar town while you shop. You can also select certain items for which the charter company may have better connections, such as good meats or vegetables from reliable suppliers. Partial provisioning also allows you to leave gaps in your meal planning for dining ashore or for discovering local foods to spice up your on-board menus.

Self-provisioning is the least expensive and takes the most effort. You buy only what you need and like, so there is little wasted food. On the other hand, your success at self-provisioning will depend on the availability of suitable markets close to the charter yacht, since you don't want to spend hours hunting for a meat market or bakery. In the Virgin Islands, there are good supermarkets in St. Thomas and Tortola that have everything you need for provisioning close to the charter bases.

Provisioning your charter boat is a task that requires both concentration and imagination. You'll want to have a shopping list prepared before you arrive, and one starting point for a self-provisioning list is the food list from the charter company itself. You'll need to remain flexible, however, in case a particular food isn't available and you have to make substitutions on the spot. If possible, key the foods on your shopping list so that you'll know not to buy certain items that were to be used in preparing a food that isn't available.

Once you've penciled out a rough menu for the week, it's time to use your imagination. Close your eyes and mentally walk through every step of preparing each meal to make sure you have all the ingredients as well as the proper utensils. For example, "Breakfast is scrambled eggs, bacon, toast and jelly . . . oops, forgot to order jelly." Another scenario might be "Dinner is barbecued steak, salad, and baked potatoes. We'll need charcoal and starter for the steak, dressing and croutons for the salad, and toppings for the potatoes. We need to order aluminum foil to bake the potatoes. Do we have matches to light the barbecue?"

When calculating the quantities you need, you should have a good idea of how your crewmembers eat. For example, are they light or heavy coffee drinkers? This can make a major difference in the amount of coffee (plus cream and sugar) that you stock. Do they like one sandwich or two for lunch? Do they want mayonnaise on their sandwiches, or butter?

Keep in mind the second uses for many foods. Lettuce, for example, is usually included for salads, but don't forget that it adds a crispness to sandwiches on a warm day, and you'll need extra heads of lettuce for that use. Cheese is good for sandwiches, but be sure you have enough for snacks as well. Plan to make use of leftovers, too. Potatoes from last night's dinner can be turned into hash browns for breakfast, while chunks of leftover meat can be used in tacos.

If you aren't familiar with an area, you should probably order a provisioning package to simplify your charter. After you've flown for hours and are faced with an unfamiliar town, perhaps another language, and a rapidly approaching departure, you may prefer to relax and simply put away the boxes on board.

Every charter company offers different provisioning packages, although they generally conform to three basic styles: a complete menu, a partial menu, or a starter kit. (Custom provisioning, of course, is available from a multipage list that can keep a gourmet cook busy for a week.)

Based on years of experience with what the charter's clients prefer (and are willing to prepare) during a charter, the complete menu usually offers enough food for every breakfast and lunch, an array of hors d'oeuvres and snacks, and dinner for several evenings, on the assumption you will dine ashore a few times.

In some areas, such as the Mediterranean, a partial menu includes only the breakfasts, lunches, and snacks, since most crews go ashore in the evenings. The starter kits usually include spices, paper towels, soap, charcoal, and other basics.

Regardless of the provisioning method, make sure that the entire crew is involved in making the choices. You should know that one of your crew hates red meat long before the provisions are ordered or the meals planned.

One charterer, who regularly sails with different crews, sends out a preference sheet for foods before starting the meal planning. The list, in chart form, covers most of the meal possibilities for breakfast, lunch, and dinner. The crewmembers then circle the items they like, and cross out the items they actively dislike. They can also number various sandwich fillings or dinner choices in order of preference.

In some locations, the charter company may stock its own provisions, in which case you can sometimes trade food from its packages. Before a charter in Baja California, for example, we swapped fish for chicken since our crewmembers weren't seafood enthusiasts, and we also traded in several cans of pears for fresh pineapples that later turned up on spears in our evening mai-tais. Keep in mind that some provisioning packages lean heavily toward steak and chicken for every dinner.

One rule is to plan simple menus, because you don't want to spend all your time in the galley. Since you may be sailing at lunchtime, the crew should be able to eat the meal one-handed while steering or simply holding on. If you're undecided about lunch menus, remember the foods that you liked as a kid. I sailed with one crewmember whose idea of heaven was peanut butter and jelly sandwiches every day.

In addition, take your charter area into account as you plan the menus. In Europe, hearty breakfasts and late dinners are the rule. In the Caribbean or South Pacific, I prefer light breakfasts, a picnic lunch ashore on an islet, and an early dinner in the cockpit as the sun sets.

Take advantage of local fruits, vegetables, and other foods, too. Bakeries, whether in St. Martin, Scotland, or the Greek Islands, can provide wonderful staples as well as delightful dessert surprises. After exploring a small village in French Polynesia, it's nearly impossible to return to the yacht without a long baguette or two of freshly baked bread and perhaps an inexpensive jug of red wine. In the Bahamas, you'll have the opportunity to buy fresh conch and lobster inexpensively. In Greece, you'll have access to fresh vegetables, lamb, and chicken.

The Caribbean in general is filled with lobster and fresh fish, but you can also sample breadfruit, mangoes, avocado, bananas, and key limes. Christophene is a local squash that can be mashed like potatoes, batter-fried like zucchini, or stuffed and baked like eggplant. Ackee grows on trees and has a custardy flesh that tastes like scrambled eggs, while Scotch Bonnet chili peppers hold the firepower of a dozen jalapeño peppers. Cassava is known to Americans as tapioca, and it can be boiled to a creamy pulp, fried into chips for spicy sauces or used in stews. If you want to try your hand at preparing some of the local foods, order a Caribbean cookbook from The Armchair Sailor bookstore (see page 111).

The converse is also true: you can't find all foods in all countries. Although it surprises many people, you cannot find tortillas in Italy for your tacos, and you'll never see maple syrup in either Portugal or French Polynesia (where you should substitute coconut syrup, anyway). Every area has local breads, but most small bakeries don't use preservatives, so keep the bread wrapped and chilled until you need it. (I've rowed a long way to bring back a sack of freshly baked warm croissants for breakfast, and you will too!)

Sailing is demanding work, so you need to have enough snacks to keep the crew stocked with munchies between scheduled meals. Salty snacks are a good idea in the tropics, where it's important to balance your loss of salts, so make sure you have enough chips, peanuts, and dips. Peanut butter is a nutritious, high-protein snack, and relatively easy to handle on crackers or celery, but it can be messy when it smears on cushions or cockpit sides. M&M's are better than chocolate bars, which can melt easily. A mix of peanuts and M&M's makes for simple handfuls of snacks, although you may find them in the corners of the cockpit if they dribble. You'll also want to have hors d'oeuvres for the cocktail hour as the dinner meal is being prepared.

Rhea Harrison, a chef who has owned several French restaurants as well as a gourmet catering company, has shown me that chartering need not be the waterborne equivalent of a Boy Scout outing, at least when it comes to food.

Rhea always takes along boneless and skinless breasts of chicken, since it is a meat acceptable to many people who don't eat red meat and it can be cooked in a thousand ways. Chicken can be sautéed, baked, broiled, fried, made into kebabs, or barbecued. The leftovers from a chicken dinner can be saved for lunch sandwiches, used in a cool dinner salad, or made into bite-sized canapés for the dinner hour.

Rhea's duffel bag usually includes a selection of her own spices from garlic to meat sauces. She also brings powdered drink mixes to simplify the cocktail hour, as well as to add some surprises. Packaged mixers, for example, can greatly simplify any drinks from mai-tais to margaritas.

By the same token, packaged fajita and taco mixes are helpful in preparing sauces and meats. Such sauces are not widely available outside the United States, so it's wise to carry them with you. They pack flat and don't take up much room.

Just because you're chartering doesn't mean you can't have some decor, so Rhea always includes a bag of tiny umbrellas for drinks, long toothpicks with colorful tops for hors d'oeuvres, and colorful straws for sipping. Her duffel bag has also included party streamers and table decor, especially if a crewmember is celebrating a birthday or there is a holiday during the voyage, and she always brings a few linen napkins to mark important meals that deserve better than paper. She picks wildflowers from shore as table decorations, and always brings a few candles for a romantic evening meal. For a seagoing chef, that's hard to beat!

When it comes to beverages, you can't have enough. A tropical climate can literally dry you out, so be sure you have an ample supply of bottled water and fruit juices. Gallon jugs of water are the least expensive but hardest to pour while sailing, so order a couple of the handier quart bottles to refill and keep chilled. When figuring out the liquids for your crew, don't include soft drinks and beer because they won't contribute much to quenching thirst. Don't forget milk, available in jugs, cartons, or canned for long life, which can be added to foods or used for a nice cup of cocoa in the evenings.

On your provisioning list, you'll be offered every beverage from Dom Perignon to cola, and you should be specific about what you are ordering and whether substitutions are acceptable to you. If you want Bloody Marys, make it clear to the charter company that they cannot substitute grape juice for tomato juice.

Alcoholic beverages are something that you can often find inexpensively during your voyage, depending once again upon the area. Local beers and wines may not be known internationally because they don't "travel" well, but you can find wonderful local wines in little European villages, and the Caribbean is notable for light and dark rums. Even in French Polynesia, where prices are sky high for restaurant foods and grocery supplies, you can find an inexpensive plastic jug of red wine that is perfectly delightful.

In some cases, hard liquor may be overly expensive and you might want to compare prices with the duty-free shops on your flight to the charter base. The Virgin Islands often have liquor price wars before Christmas, and you should always shop around if your first quote seems high.

General Tips

After stowing your foods, put the cardboard grocery boxes ashore, since cockroaches like the glue found in the corrugations and can get aboard that way. Once you've opened a package or box of food, seal it closed inside a Ziploc bag to prevent any spillage, and keep bugs and moisture out.

Ice in most areas is a suitable substitute for gold, so carry plenty. I usually ask for a spare ice chest filled with bags of ice cubes, which can be stowed under the dining table or in the lazarette. Use the ice judiciously in drinks or to keep beer and soft drink cans cold.

If you expect the day's sail to be boisterous, you may not want to be down below in the galley while the boat is gyrating around you. Make up sandwiches in the morning, wrap them in plastic for freshness, and store them in the refrigerator in a bag along with chips or nuts. When the crew gets hungry, you can send the one with the strongest stomach below to retrieve lunch.

Most charter yachts have areas set aside as "liquor lockers," often with cutouts for bottle storage, but you should be careful when stowing glass bottles. Make sure they don't clank into each other, and store wine bottles upright to prevent leakage after opening. Some vintage wines suffer from disturbed sediment when taken sailing, so be selective in your choices. (Champagne, incidentally, sails very well.)

Your first chore when you arrive at your charter boat is to empty the cardboard cartons of food into the lockers below.

In general, try to keep all lunch foods (or foods to be eaten while under way) as simple as possible. A sailing meal shouldn't be easy to spill, leave the hands greasy, or take more than one hand to eat.

If possible, keep all the canned drinks in one side of the refrigerator, and the foods in another, since the crew will be in and out constantly. It's even better to put the drinks in a separate ice chest and restock it daily.

Wrap lettuce, celery, and other vegetables tightly in plastic wrap to keep them from getting limp in the refrigerator.

Paper plates simplify clean-up immensely, but they're generally too flimsy for anything but sandwiches. Instead, you can use paper plates on top of your regular plates for strength and simplicity. An alternative is to bring a set of lightweight rattan paper-plate liners from home, which are decorative as well as sturdy.

While using the stove, remember that even in a calm anchorage a passing boat can cause your boat to lurch, so protect yourself from splatters and spills. Use the fiddles (adjustable brackets) to keep pots from sliding on the stove. As one experienced sailor warned, "Don't fry bacon in your birthday suit," and that applies to skimpy bathing suits as well.

Carry plenty of plastic bags in various sizes for storing food, saving leftovers, and freezing fresh-caught fish for later use. If you want special spices or condiments, put them in plastic bags and bring them from home, but be prepared to explain to immigration that the whitish substance is just garlic powder.

Trash bags not only store garbage, but also keep your cameras and wallets dry when going ashore by dinghy. If you find the trash beginning to ripen, simply put the garbage bag in the dinghy to keep the yacht smelling fresh.

If you have favorite cooking knives, you might want to bring them from home, since you never know what you'll find aboard the boat. Some cooks simply bring a small sharpening stone, because they've found that charter yacht knives are uniformly dull from cutting lines, cleaning fish, and other such treatment.

As a precaution, you might want to throw in a couple of rolls of antacid tablets to combat spicy meals ashore.

Sample Menus

Just because you're off cruising doesn't mean you have to suffer, and the following meals have proven over the years to be simple to prepare and a pleasure to eat.

Breakfasts

>   Scrambled eggs, bacon, toast, and fresh fruit
>   French toast, fresh peaches with cream
>   Cereal with sugar, milk, sliced bananas
>   Potato pancakes with sour cream and salsa
>   Omelettes, croissants, and fruit
>   Fresh fruit, French bread, and cheese
>   Poached eggs, corned beef hash, muffins, and fruit
>   Pancakes with syrup, melon

Lunches

Tuna salad, chips and salsa
Beef tacos (leftover beef) with cheese, sour cream, avocado, and refried beans
Chicken sandwiches (leftover chicken) with Swiss cheese and avocado
Pasta salad
Grilled cheese sandwiches

Dinners

Barbecued steak, green salad, hot-fudge sundaes
Roast beef, mashed potatoes, green beans amandine, apple pie

A permanently mounted table in the cockpit is a bonus: dining alfresco is pleasant in most charter areas, and a table also simplifies snacks while under way.

Chicken breast sautéed in marsala, rice, green salad, chocolate cake

Broiled lamb chops with red wine, potatoes, asparagus, ice cream

Scallops, mushrooms, shallots sautéed in butter, squash, pudding

Spaghetti with meat sauce, garlic bread, spinach salad, rum cake

LIVING ABOARD

A charter yacht is not unlike a small mountain cabin or a beach cottage, and spending a week there in close proximity to other people requires some flexibility, humor, and resourcefulness. Privacy, silence, and water are often in short supply, so you should prize all three things highly. The remaining items in this chapter are arranged in no particular order, although all are important for a pleasant cruise.

Water

Water surrounds you, of course, but drinking water is a commodity that you must conserve carefully. Treat it like gold because, in many charter areas, it is priced similarly if you can get it at all.

Most charter yachts have shower heads that can be switched off once you have the temperature set. The procedure, sometimes called "Navy showers," is to wet yourself down and then turn off the water. Use your shampoo and soap to lather up completely, then flick the shower button on for a quick rinse to remove the soap. When shaving, fill the sink with warm water rather than running the water over your razor.

In the galley, you're likely to have both a freshwater faucet and a foot-operated saltwater pump. Use saltwater for a preliminary cleaning of the dishes and utensils, then rinse them in freshwater. You can also use saltwater if you need boiling water for thawing foods.

The Toilet

It is absolutely essential that everyone aboard understands how to operate a marine toilet, or head as it is called. During the checkout, you should have everyone practice flushing while there is someone present from the charter company. It is possible to exist on a charter boat without a functioning toilet, but it is not a pleasant experience.

Be sure that you have an ample supply of the proper toilet paper, since marine toilets are finicky that way. And don't put anything in the toilet that you haven't eaten first. It's that simple.

Every charter yacht will have a scrub brush and cleanser so you can keep the toilet clean, and this is everyone's responsibility. To keep the head fresh, men should sit rather than stand when using the typically small marine toilets, especially when the weather is rough.

The head compartment on this yacht provides lockers for toiletries, along with a vanity and large mirror.

The Refrigerator

Because most charter cruising areas are located in warm climates, keeping food cold is a high priority, for the health and comfort of the crew. Many charter yachts have a compressor-driven refrigeration system that operates only when the engine is running, so be sure to ask during your checkout about the amount of engine time needed to keep the refrigerator cold.

Packing a refrigerator is a science and an art, but it's not difficult. The coldest area of the refrigerator is near the cold plates, so you should put frozen foods and supplies you don't need until the end of the cruise there. Be sure that frozen foods are wrapped carefully to avoid freezer burn, since some island groceries are casual about packaging. Rewrap any meat packaged in plastic shrink-wrap, since it is too thin to provide adequate protection.

If you have an icebox, empty out the melt water regularly, because ice melts more quickly when standing in water. You might want to save this water for cooking or shaving, too.

Open the refrigerator as infrequently as you can to preserve the cold. If you remove food that you plan to return to the refrigerator, do it as quickly as you can so it stays cold.

Many charter companies provide an ice chest in addition to the refrigerator, and you can use this for soft drinks, beer, and juices that you'll want all day long.

Privacy

One of the pleasures of a charter cruise is the ability to curl up in perfect surroundings and enjoy some peace . . . from children, from work, and even from friends. Think twice before you plop down and start talking to someone who is obviously engrossed in a book.

By the same token, each stateroom is sacrosanct and, unless you've been invited to enter or asked to fetch something, stay out! Somehow, many of the common sensibilities found in homes are left behind on a charter, and you need to consciously respect the privacy of others. In a private home, you wouldn't walk unannounced into someone's bedroom, so don't do it on a boat.

Privacy also applies to other yachts, and you must never, ever, board another yacht uninvited (except when rafted alongside). If you want to visit a neighboring boat, bring your dinghy alongside and shout "ahoy," which gives the crew time to hide the dirty dishes before responding.

If you find yourself rafted up next to another boat and need to cross its deck to get ashore, always follow the same rules as you would at home. Use the foredeck (which is the front yard) rather than tramping through the cockpit (which is the living room).

Last, if you have rambunctious children aboard, plan to run the engine or generator often, or if you want to play your radio loudly, find an anchoring area away from your neighbors.

Stowage

One simple rule covers every situation: put things away. This sounds like your mother nagging at you to pick up your room, but on an already confined charter boat, it takes only a few items strewn around to create a pigpen. Leaving towels, jackets, books, or camera bags on the settees below or in the cockpit not only prevents other people from using those areas, but also could prove dangerous if someone trips or slips.

Before setting out for the day's voyage, secure everything down below, make sure that all the locker doors are closed and locked, and that there are no loose items that can fall when the boat heels to the first puff of wind. At the same time, close all the portholes until you're certain that there won't be any spray on deck. A wet bunk makes for a very unhappy shipmate.

As a matter of course, you'll be using the lifelines as a clothesline (remember to bring clothespins) to dry towels and swimsuits, but these should all be put away before you depart, or you'll stand a chance of watching your dry clothes disappear overboard.

Batteries

Most charter yachts have their electrical systems arranged so that one battery is used solely for starting the engine, and one or more other batteries supply the power for lights, refrigeration, water pressure pumps, and so forth. If you treat electricity as if it were freshwater and always turn everything off when not needed, you'll never have electrical problems of your own causing.

During the checkout, make sure you understand the various positions of the master battery switch, since leaving it in the wrong position can leave you without enough battery power to crank the engine.

Clearance

When entering a country, you need to clear through immigration as soon as possible. In many charter areas, this is a casual affair in which visitors simply anchor off the nearest town and search out the local officials, whose offices are usually near the docks. Elsewhere, a more traditional method may be used. In some areas, you might need to call the customs or health officials on VHF radio and request that they come to your yacht, or you may indicate the same need by flying the yellow Q, or quarantine, flag from the starboard spreader after anchoring.

Requirements and formalities vary. Some countries require a typed list (in triplicate) of your crew, as well as a look at the ship's papers, all passports, and a copy of your clearance papers from the last port of call. Others may simply want to stamp your passports, and a few don't bother with any of this.

During your briefing, be sure to ask about the formalities for any foreign waters that you plan to cruise. If necessary, the charter company can provide you with the properly typed lists or forms required in each area.

Flags

It is common courtesy as well as a requirement in many areas that you not only fly the national ensign of the country in which your yacht is registered, but also fly the courtesy flag of the country being visited. In some areas, officials (particularly in emerging nations) have become most inhospitable to yachts that do not observe this courtesy. On most charter yachts, you'll find an array of foreign flags in the navigation table, usually marked so you know which is which. The courtesy flag should be flown from the starboard spreader after you have cleared into the country and lowered the Q flag.

If you are a member of a yacht club, you can take your burgee with you and fly it from the starboard spreader if you are unable to attach it to the masthead in the traditional location.

Money

The American dollar is accepted in most parts of the world, particularly in the Caribbean, although you're likely to receive your change in the local currency, such as French francs or Dutch guilders.

Unless you're a long way out in the boondocks, traveler's checks are easily cashed, but I always carry a wad of dollar bills and some local currency that I converted at the airport or at a local bank. That way, I've covered for the miscellaneous costs and tips that come along.

When it comes to sharing the finances, you need to be clear with the others in the crew about how to deal with expenses. Certainly if you go ashore, you're on your own for food, drink, and any other purchases. But what if you buy food for the boat?

I've found that a "kitty" in the form of a plastic bag taped to the chart table can be the solution. Each crewmember puts in $20 at the start of the trip, and this kitty is used to pay for mooring charges, customs fees, for additional food, or even to tip the boat boys. When the bag runs dry, everyone puts in another $20 to top it up. When the occasion seems appropriate, this kitty might also be used (by common consent) to treat everyone to ice cream cones or a round of drinks ashore.

Drugs

Don't even think about taking any recreational drugs on a charter boat. If you weren't thoroughly frightened by the movie *Midnight*

Express, then remember that the only penalty for drugs in some cruising areas is execution. No appeals, no delays.

BARBECUES

Nearly every charter yacht has a barbecue mounted to the stern pulpit, since it's a perfect way to grill dinner while enjoying the sunset and cockpit conversation. Take some simple precautions, because this is an open fire.

First, make sure no lines are dangling nearby that can blow into the fire on an errant puff. Until you've seen a synthetic line catch fire like a firecracker fuse, you won't believe how flammable it is. The same applies to the bimini top and sail cover, which should be out of the way.

In a breeze, sparks can fly, and although your boat is usually safe since the stern is downwind at anchor, the sparks may scatter over yachts anchored astern of you, so keep an eye open for stray embers. Most charter companies insist that you use only charcoal and lighter fluid, but there's always someone who uses newspaper that floats off to leeward as a miniature firebomb.

If you can't seal off the top of the barbecue to starve the fire of oxygen after cooking is completed, dump the charcoal into the water and make sure that all embers are out. An untended barbecue is an invitation to trouble.

HALYARDS

There are few sounds as irritating in an otherwise quiet anchorage as the bong-bong-bong of your neighbor's halyards slapping against a hollow aluminum mast.

Even if it doesn't bother you, your neighbors may not be pleased, so tie your halyards away from the mast as part of the postanchoring clean-up drill. In too many instances, a crew drops sail, lowers the anchor, and jumps in the dinghy to explore ashore without bothering even to casually tie off the halyards. These thoughtless types have returned to find all of the loose halyards pulled to the top of the mast. The effort to retrieve those halyards usually serves to teach the lesson.

Generators

Right up there in the same category as noisy halyards are noisy generators that run continuously. If you must use a generator, whether you are on a powerboat or a sailboat, use it sparingly. Cook your meal with the electric oven, chill the cabin down with the air conditioning, and then turn the generator off. If you must run the generator all night long, find another anchorage away from everyone else. There have been instances of charter crews going ashore and leaving the generator running endlessly into the evening, only to return to a yacht silenced by a potato shoved into the generator exhaust.

Garbage

You'll probably be told where to dump garbage during your pre-charter briefing. If not, be sure to ask. Nearly every charter area has designated garbage collection sites, and it seems redundant in this ecologically conscious era to have to emphasize that no garbage should be dumped overboard.

Carry a supply of large plastic trash bags with strong ties, and seal your garbage in these regularly to keep the cabin smelling fresh. There is often storage space in the lazarette or cockpit lockers to hide the filled trash bags until you can find a place to dump them.

Most towns that cater to charterers have dump bins near the docks for trash, but a few require a small fee for use.

Bugs

You can expect to encounter various irritating critters of one kind or another during your cruise, so be prepared for them beforehand. Mosquitos, gnats, or the ubiquitous "no-see-ums" are particularly annoying when they circle your face at three in the morning.

If you expect to encounter insects, bring repellent spray or lotion from home that you have tested and found to be effective. Even if you don't expect to encounter insects, bring one can of repellent anyway, because you never know when you'll need it.

One popular cure for flying insects is to use Avon's Skin So Soft body lotion, which makes humans soft and pleasant smelling but is apparently a bane to nearly every insect.

Roaches can also be found on charter yachts, although most companies fumigate regularly to keep them to a minimum. Start with a dose of prevention, and don't bring any cardboard boxes on board, since roaches can hide in the corrugations. Inspect boxes and can labels for roach eggs, which look like a dark blob of syrup about the size of a teardrop.

While there are a number of commercial roach sprays and poisons, the most effective aboard a boat seems to be a sprinkling of borax (such as found in Boraxo cleanser) in the bilge, locker bottoms, and in cabinets.

Sharing

Remember that a charter cruise is a group effort, so be sure to share in the duties and responsibilities whenever you can. If you aren't a good cook, you might volunteer for the galley clean-up duties, or you can make the lunch sandwiches. On a recent charter out of St. Martin, the mainsail was so hard to hoist that we ended up giving each male crewmember a "mainsail day," when his task was to raise the main instead of helping with the anchor.

Children

Bareboat chartering is a wonderful experience for children and it can be equally wonderful for the parents (and other crew), or it can be a frantic, noisy, and harried existence with no escape.

Safety is probably the biggest concern of any parent, particularly on a sailboat with a variety of potentially dangerous equipment surrounded by deep water.

Your first step should be to make sure that your child is a good swimmer, which usually means Red Cross swimming courses at an early age. Young children should also wear life jackets on deck and in the cockpit; these can be the comfortable vest styles that don't inhibit movement. Parents should also consider using a safety harness whenever the child is on deck while the boat is under way. Always know where your children are on the boat. Under sail, bright-colored clothing is a good idea. Show your children any potential hazards such as the anchor windlass, and warn them of the dangers in language that they can understand.

Because the parents may not be in command of the boat, be sure that children understand that the skipper's commands must be obeyed completely and immediately, just as though the orders were from the parents. As in any nautical situation, the captain's word is law.

If adults have trouble with sunburn, it should come as no surprise that children are even more susceptible. Long-sleeved shirts and lots of sun protection are necessary to avoid a painful burn.

Carry extra clothing, since kids are likely to get wet more often than adults. Spray from the bow is the seagoing equivalent of mud puddles, and you can count on children to frolic in it.

Children should also be given tasks during the charter, both to keep their interest and to involve them in the group activity. Trimming a jib sheet may be too much for their strength, but don't be afraid to let them try—it's part of the learning process. Besides, once they learn the loads that are involved, they'll be much more cautious in the future.

The one area that fascinates children is steering and, in most conditions, it's something they can do easily. They'll make mistakes, but your patience can lead to a fulfilling experience for them. Kids also like to study charts and delight in spotting buoys long before the adults. They can also help by watching the depth sounder in shallow waters, by coiling lines and halyards, and by tending the dinghy when everyone else is busy.

Kids will want to explore all parts of the boat, sit on the main boom, and swing on the rigging. Most of the time this is fine, but it may be too much during cocktail hour or early in the morning.

You should plan to bring a bag of distractions, such as a book of knots with some lengths of light line for practice, or cards, checkers, and puzzles. A pocket tape player (with earphones, of course) and some story tapes suitable for the children can entertain them and provide quiet time for parents and crew alike.

CHARTER AREAS

CARIBBEAN

*W*ithout a doubt, the Caribbean is the most popular charter area in the world. Every major charter company has at least one and often several bases scattered through this island chain. The Caribbean is a drawing card not just for Americans fleeing the winter slush, but also for huge numbers of French, English, Italians, and other Europeans who enjoy the international flavor of these multination islands.

Your atlas will give you the details, but this cruising ground is essentially a long string of islands stretching through a crescent that curves east and south from Florida to the Venezuelan coast, forming a natural barrier between the Atlantic Ocean and the Caribbean Sea.

Because of the warm winds, protected waterways, and safe anchorages, this island necklace draws beginning and expert sailors alike. Chartering is a major tourist industry, attracting jet loads full of sailors from around the world. As a result, these are also the most congested charter waters to be found. The only drawback to the Caribbean is that too many sailors know about it.

But don't let that dissuade you, or you'll miss an ocean full of treasures ranging from tiny coral atolls to brooding foliage-covered volcanic islands laced with perfect beaches and harbors. In fact, a day's passage between many of these islands can bring a completely different culture: from British colonialism to Swedish architecture, from Dutch accents to American fast foods.

The Greater Antilles start just ninety miles off the Florida coast with Cuba, Jamaica, Haiti, the Dominican Republic, and Puerto Rico. East of Puerto Rico are the Virgin Islands, and then an open-water gap to Anguilla, which begins the Lesser Antilles. Stretching more than four hundred miles to the South American coast, the Lesser Antilles were divided by the British into the Leeward and the Windward Islands, although more for governmental reasons than geographic ones.

The Leeward Islands range from St. Martin and Anguilla to Dominica, while the Windwards lie southward from Martinique to Grenada. In addition, charterers are beginning to explore the Dutch "ABCs" (Aruba, Bonaire, and Curaçao) off the Venezuelan coast, as well as the reefs of Belize at the far western corner of the Caribbean.

Bear in mind the above names for the various areas, because you'll also hear a wide variety of other names that often seem confusing. The French Antilles are those islands clustered around Guadeloupe, while the Grenadines are the islands from St. Vincent to Grenada. But the Dutch islands of Saba, St. Martin, and Statia are sometimes called the Dutch Windwards, even though they are a part of the Leeward Islands. To compound things, St. Martin is often written as St. Maarten since it is half Dutch, and the islands of St. Barthélemy and St. Eustatius are usually shortened to St. Barts and Statia.

Weather: The prime charter season is mid-December through March, when most North Americans and Europeans are looking for escapes from winter snow and cold. The weather can be variable at that time, however, with rain squalls and strong breezes.

For the Caribbean, northeasterly tradewinds are the most common, ranging mostly from east to east northeast. Wind speed in the eighteen- to twenty-five-knot range is the norm for the winter months, while summer breezes drop to the low teens. The exceptions are the so-called "Christmas Winds" that often whistle more than thirty-five knots on short notice. In general, you can expect the strongest breezes in the Windward Islands, and the easiest sailing in the Virgins.

The best sailing season is from April through July, when the winds are lighter but steady from the east to southeast, and the weather is more predictable. Rain falls year-round, although steady rain is rare. Instead, you can watch the big cumulus clouds build into towers and see the rain squalls slanting under each one, bringing short bursts of heavy rain followed by rainbows and clear skies.

The hurricane season is theoretically from late July through early October, although off-season hurricanes are not uncommon. The hurricane season is usually the least expensive for chartering; some companies offer two weeks for the price of one. Often the weather is flawless, but you run the risk not only of hurricanes but also of fitful winds that can die suddenly, leaving you melting in high humidity. Keep in mind that hurricanes are more likely to hit the East Coast of the United States than they are to rumble through the Caribbean.

While there are a number of reasonably protected areas (such as much of the Virgin Islands and the Tobago Cays), the other island areas are exposed to Atlantic swells that have been pushed all the way from Africa by the tradewinds, so the seas on many passages can be aggressive.

Books have been written about each of these island groups, so I'll skim over each of the major charter areas and suggest those sights that I've enjoyed.

THE VIRGIN ISLANDS

While the Caribbean is the most popular charter region in the world, the Virgin Islands are easily the most popular area within the Caribbean. Divided in half, with the U.S. Virgins to the west and the British Virgins to the east, this charter area is roughly forty-five miles long by about fifteen miles wide, so you can cover much of it in an afternoon sail.

The Virgins, both U.S. and British, are a first-timer's paradise: The islands are close together, which makes for smooth water sailing. The area is dotted with anchorages, many with mooring buoys, and the only drawback to the region is that it's too popular.

Spiced with tales of Henry Morgan, Bluebeard, corsairs, and yellowed treasure maps, the majority of the sailing takes place in channels protected from the big Atlantic swells and navigation is entirely by eye. Accordingly, the Virgins are an ideal spot to test your newly found chartering skills. In fact, you're never out of sight of land in the Virgins, and many of the anchorages are within a few miles of each other, leaving plenty of time to explore or sail before anchoring for the night. The water is clear to remarkable depths, and the weather is generally settled.

The British Virgins (usually called BVI) have more charter boats than the American islands, with several large companies based on Tortola, which is centrally located in the middle of the

The harbor at Charlotte Amalie in the U.S. Virgin Islands is pretty but often filled with cruise ships. (Photo courtesy U.S. Virgin Islands Division of Tourism)

chain. In fact, The Moorings advertises that more than sixteen anchorages are within one hour's sail from their marina in Road Town, and an equal number are probably within reach of other charter company bases at Red Hook or East End.

On a typical itinerary from Tortola, many boats start their cruises by reaching south across Sir Francis Drake Channel to The Bight on Norman Island, a completely protected anchorage with a good breeze for air conditioning. As a result, The Bight is often congested but still worth a visit, since nearby caves are said to be those described in Robert Louis Stevenson's *Treasure Island* and, in fact, treasure has been found in the area.

Virgin Gorda is another popular site on the charter trail, particularly The Baths at the southern tip, which are a giant's playground of huge boulders tumbled over each other at the water's edge. The result is a series of interconnected grottoes of cool, clear water, marked by intricate patterns of sunlight shining through gaps in the boulders and reflecting around the pools. Since The Baths can often be overrun by tourists and other charter yachts, you might prefer nearby Devil's Bay, which has similar boulders, a nicer beach, and no crowds.

At the opposite end of the island is Gorda Sound, another protected area with numerous anchorages as well as a collection of excellent restaurants for evening dining. Also located in Gorda Sound and accessible only by water is the Bitter End Yacht Club, a private resort on Mosquito Island that welcomes sailors.

On the Atlantic side of Tortola is Cane Garden Bay, said to be the prettiest cove in the world, which is an excellent anchorage except in northerly winds. Be sure to try Stanley Hodges's Welcome Bar and Restaurant for great lobster, music, and rum drinks. Nearby is the Callwood distillery, where you can sample the island rum. But beware, it's strong stuff.

For divers or snorkelers, try Salt Island, where the Royal Mail Ship *Rhone* sank during a storm in 1876 and whose remains are now a condo for brightly colored fish.

Moorings have been set by a private firm both as a commercial operation and to help protect the coral reefs, which have been damaged by inconsiderate anchoring. The moorings, which cost

$15 per night, are located at Cooper Island, Drake's Anchorage, and Vixen Point in Virgin Gorda's North Sound, Cane Garden Bay, Soper's Hole, and in two areas of Little Harbor on Jost van Dyke.

The U.S. Virgin Islands were acquired from the Danes in 1917 and parts of it still retain a European flavor, including the habit of driving on the left. The capital, Charlotte Amalie, is packed to bursting with cruise ships and tourists, however, and crime is becoming enough of a problem that most charter boats not based in the harbor tend to skip this city. It also includes fast-food chains and shops filled with tourist junk, from which most charterers are trying to escape.

Red Hook Bay on the east side of St. Thomas is a major charter base and is a convenient starting point for exploring the British Virgins. Be sure to clear customs on the way out and back, or you'll pay a fine.

Nearby St. John is often overlooked by sailors in a hurry to reach the British Virgins, but it offers some delights of its own. Most of it is a national park, so it remains untouched and original, and the rest of the island is equally distant from the twentieth century. Cruz Bay, where you'll clear customs, is often congested, but Pusser's Pub, which serves rum of the same name, is both nautical and scenic. Caneel Bay on the

Trunk Bay on St. John in the U.S. Virgin Islands is a popular spot for swimming and snorkeling.

north side of the island is a posh Rockefeller resort that requires coats and ties, so many charterers skip that area, but you might try Honeymoon Beach just west of Caneel Bay, where tame manta rays are often found playing in shallow water. Another prime snorkeling area is Haulover Bay at the eastern tip of St. John, with giant pillars of elkhorn coral heads.

The Leeward Islands

Made up of the primary islands of St. Martin, Anguilla, St. Barts, St. Kitts, Guadeloupe, and Dominica, plus a collection of smaller islets, this is a fascinating mix of British, Dutch, French, and West Indian cultures. Sailing the Leewards involves some open water passages that can be challenging, and is more appropriate for experienced sailors. Because they required an often nasty beat in sloppy head seas from the Virgin Islands, the northernmost of the Leewards were late bloomers in the charter business.

St. Martin/St. Maarten is a unique combination of Paris and Amsterdam spiced with West Indian rhythms. Visited by Columbus, it was a battlefield until the seventeenth century when France and the Netherlands agreed to split the island in half. Several major charter operations are based here, and among the many spectacular anchorages are Simpson Bay, Marcel Bay, Grand Case, and Orient Bay. Marigot, the French capital, has chic shops and waterfront cafes where you can munch on a croissant and stock up on red wine. The Dutch capital, Philipsburg, also has shopping, casinos, and nightlife, but the anchorage is often too lumpy for comfortable overnight stays. St. Martin has become one of the largest charter bases in the Caribbean, in part because the French offer tremendous tax advantages to those who invest in charter boats.

Anguilla, just five miles away, remains British. This low coral island is largely undeveloped, so the white-sand beaches and offshore reefs remain unspoiled. Road Bay is a pleasant anchorage, although you'll hear all the revelry at Johnny O's on the beach. Don't miss out on the "conch lady" at the end of the beach, who has a mountain of conch shells for sale at reasonable prices. At

St. Martin's Anse Marcel combines charter bases for several companies with a luxury resort facility that allows charterers to arrive early or depart late.

nearby Prickly Pear Cays, you'll find some of the best snorkeling in the Caribbean, with several sunken ships to spice up the view. Sandy Cay, just offshore from Road Bay, is everyone's idea of a tiny tropical island, and you can pick up a mooring outside the reef for a daytime stop, although it's usually too turbulent for overnighting. There's a tiny snack bar ashore, and an inviting reef that surrounds the palm-fringed islet. Anguilla has instituted a rather hefty "cruising fee" on charter yachts that ranges up to $125 per day, depending upon the size of the yacht. Check with your charter company to see if the fee has been paid by it or repealed.

St. Barts is French, and has become a jet-set destination, which hasn't helped prices or service particularly. Named by Columbus for his brother, it has a couple of good anchorages. The port of Gustavia on the west coast is protected and charming, but often packed to the gills with visiting yachts paying $14 to Med moor to the quay. Because it is so sheltered, however, it can also be hot and humid. Food is a way of life to the French, so tiny St. Barts (with a population of just three thousand) has more than seventy restaurants, and you can also find jazz and dancing until the wee hours. As a bonus, the French officials are good natured and helpful.

Saba is about twenty-five miles southwest of St. Martin but rarely visited by charter yachts because it has no harbors. To land, you must pick very calm weather to use the pier.

Statia is pretty, with clouds usually snagged on its peak, but has little to draw charterers since the anchorages are open and lumpy. St. Kitts and Nevis are also pretty, but also have uncomfortable anchorages.

Antigua was where chartering began in the Caribbean, with yachts based at English Harbour, so named because Lord Nelson kept his British fleet here while colonizing North America. The British flavor remains, from the cannons on display to the seawall filled with yachts.

Each spring, Antigua hosts Antigua Race Week, an event that draws sailors and camp followers from around the world to a week of offshore sailing and onshore hijinks. Unless you plan to sail or participate in wet T-shirt contests, this is a good time to stay away from Antigua because of the crowds and high prices.

Try to arrive in English Harbour on a Sunday, because the entire island seems to cab or hike up to Shirley Heights for the sunset and view of other islands, and then to enjoy cocktails and a barbecue, followed by steel bands and reggae music.

There's more to Antigua than just English Harbour, however, and locals claim that the island has one beach for every day of the year. There are also a number of pleasant coves and anchorages, and some charterers never leave the island, contenting themselves to simply cruise from one anchorage to another. Good anchorages include Five Islands, Deep Bay, Mosquito Cove, and Dickenson Bay. Sailing along the leeward side is unforgettable, with good breezes, no swells, and crystal clear water that reveals the bottom thirty feet below.

Guadeloupe is actually two islands (Basse-Terre and Grand-Terre) that are connected by a drawbridge. Basse-Terre has a lush 60,000-acre national park complete with 300-foot waterfall as well as an underwater park (near Pigeon Island) named by Jacques Cousteau as one of the world's ten best diving areas. Just south are Les Saintes (The Saints), a cluster of islands that have become a popular vacation spot for local residents, so the anchorages are sometimes crowded and rumpled by passing ferries.

A four-to-five-hour sail from Guadeloupe, Dominica is one of the most exotic of the Caribbean islands, with a lush tropical rainforest, bamboo forests, and a mountain that towers more than a mile high. You can easily spend a day with a local guide exploring the interior of the island, since there are more than 350 rivers and spectacular scenery. It also has fewer harbors than other islands, although the best is Prince Rupert Bay. A word of warning, however: the geography at the entrance to the harbor creates some ferocious wind gusts, although the seas remain smooth. You'll also find boats full of boys who insist on helping you. Once you've picked "your" boy (negotiate all fees beforehand!), he'll chase the others away, watch your boat for you, and deliver ice or fruit from shore. He may also offer to lead you up Indian River by dinghy, which is a fun trip into a lush jungle where you can swim in clear freshwater.

The Windward Islands

Martinique is another base for charter operators, and this big French island is topped by Mt. Pelée at the south end, a hulking volcano that wiped out a town of 40,000 (except for one prisoner in the dungeon) with an eruption in 1902. The largest city, Fort-de-France, is a favorite stop for cruise ships, so the bay can be lumpy and crowded. St. Ann is a pleasant little town with a good anchorage as well as shops and restaurants. Anse d'Arlet is a lovely anchorage in front of a French fishing village, and Anse Mitan has beach restaurants and a casino.

St. Lucia is also a charter base, and James Michener called Marigot Bay "the most beautiful bay in the Caribbean." Equally beautiful are The Pitons, a pair of lush twin peaks 2700 feet high, and you should take advantage of the palm-fringed anchorage with black sand beaches (Anse de Piton) nearby. If you can, anchor bow out and put a stern line to a palm tree, but make sure everything is secure, because the Pitons can generate some fierce wind gusts occasionally. Rodney Bay is another secure harbor, and a complete marina facility has shops, boutiques, and sprawling lawns.

St. Vincent is not particularly popular with charterers since some of the locals, from boat boys to officials, can be irritatingly rude, and the scenic sight on the island is the extensive Botanical Gardens.

THE GRENADINES

Technically the Grenadines are part of the Windward Islands, but most charter brochures list them separately, so I'm giving in to common usage.

The Grenadines, which stretch from St. Vincent to Grenada, are politically divided: St. Vincent owns those south to Mustique, while Grenada owns the remaining islands. With dozens of lovely anchorages, many charterers swear that a ten-day charter should be the minimum for this area. Ideally, a one-way charter allows you to explore the entire area at leisure, rather than retracing your steps, and some charter companies offer this option.

Because the harbor at Kingstown on St. Vincent is usually rough (and because the natives are not always pleasant), most yachtsmen skip the island and enter the Grenadines at Bequia (pronounced *beck*-wee).

Bequia's main harbor, Admiralty Bay, is usually filled with yachts, and boats are built along the beachfront. Expect to be set upon by souvenir-sellers and musicians who arrive by boat and, if you go ashore, be sure to tip the youngsters who offer to guard your dinghy (no more than five dollars EC), or you'll find it cast adrift. On the east side of the island is Friendship Bay, a throwback to *Moby Dick* where the locals hunt whales (in oar-powered longboats) from January through March.

Mustique is best known for its jet set, including Princess Margaret, Raquel Welch, and Mick Jagger, who own property here.

The attraction of this island is the snorkeling and, just off the north coast, the wreck of the ocean liner *Antilles*. The only good anchorage on Mustique is Britannia Bay, which also has Basil's Bar for rum punches and fabulous lobster dinners.

Cannouan Island is an overlooked prize, since it is usually missed by bareboaters intent on getting farther south. Charlestown Bay has interesting ruins to explore and, if you're a snorkeler, be sure to hire a guide to pilot your boat around to the east side, where the reefs are spectacular.

The Tobago Cays are the jewels of the Grenadines, and the reason that many charterers return over and over again. Hidden from the Atlantic behind World's End and Horseshoe Reefs, these four islands are probably the most photographed beaches and coves in the Caribbean. Since they are uninhabited and have easily navigated deep-water channels, you can spend days wandering from one white beach to the next. At the height of the midwinter charter season they can get busy, but there's always enough space for a few more yachts. The snorkeling on the reefs is fabulous and, on the beaches, you can easily find too many shells to keep. Your dinghy will get a real workout, as there's something to see in all directions. In good weather you can anchor offshore at World's End Reef, a particularly appropriate name since there is no land between it and Africa or Europe.

Just west of the Cays is Mayreau, with the wreck of a WWI gunboat just offshore for divers to explore and Dennis' Hideaway for delicious garlic-steamed lobster and conch fritters. Salt Whistle Bay is a protected and spectacular half-moon anchorage with a white sandy beach and shallow reefs for exploring on each side. Many cruising sailors say that Salt Whistle is the prettiest anchorage in the world. Don't be put off by the guidebooks that describe the reefs as dangerous. The reefs and rocks are plainly visible with ample room between them.

Union Island can be tricky, with a reef on the southern side, but Chatham Bay on the northwest side is protected and often deserted. Clifton Harbor is well protected even in bad weather, but watch out for the unmarked reef just offshore.

Carriacou is a leisurely island of boat builders and a hundred rum shops, with Tyrell Bay serving as a respite from the strong currents and sometimes rough seas found between Grenada and Carriacou, which also have the strange and craggy rocks called The Sisters and Kick 'Em Jenny.

Grenada is best known for the American "rescue mission" in the early 1980s, but it has since settled down and is one of the most picturesque islands in the Windwards. The best cruising is on the southwestern coast. You may end up motor sailing because the mountains often block the breeze, but you can spend a week exploring the coves and beaches.

The harbor at St. George's used to be one of the few places to see banana boats and trading schooners and, in addition to clearing in or out of the islands here, you can provision at the Foodland store right by the dinghy dock. The town is also pretty, with pastel houses rising up into the hillsides around the harbor. Prickly Bay at the south end has several charter bases and is a good anchorage to start an exploration of the many southern bays. Grenada has earned its nickname as The Spice Island and, sailing close to shore

St. George's is the capital of Grenada and one of the most picturesque ports in the Caribbean.

after a rain squall, you can actually smell the nutmeg. If you want to get off the boat for a day, take a tour of the island, where everything grows profusely and there are some waterfalls in the mountains.

One last note about Caribbean chartering for sailors who like to cruise but miss the racing action they left at home: a growing number of regattas are being held throughout the Caribbean that not only permit but actually encourage bareboat charter entrants with separate classes.

The oldest and certainly most renowned is the previously mentioned Antigua Sailing Week every April, which has grown for over two decades. The pace at Antigua involves an early afternoon race (which includes everything from maxi-boats to classic schooners), followed by beach activities such as inflatable races and wet T-shirt (or less) contests. In the evenings, the parties seem to go on endlessly, or at least that's how long the drums last.

Also in April are the Rolex Cup and the British Virgin Islands Regatta, both in BVI. While the waters are smoother, the racing is even more hard-fought than at Antigua, particularly during the Rolex Cup when the prizes are watches. Other fast-growing events include the Heineken-sponsored regatta at St. Martin in March and the St. Barts Regatta in February.

NorthSouth Charters, based in British Virgin Gorda, has organized its own regatta called the Canadian Challenge, which features three days of racing aboard a dozen C&C 41s, leaving time in the week-long package to explore the area as well. Steve Colgate's Offshore Sailing School has also scheduled a "Sailmaker's Caribbean Challenge" aboard a fleet of Moorings 38s for point-to-point racing through the British Virgin Islands, with a coach from a major sail loft aboard each yacht to share racing insights. The Moorings has its own one-design regatta in the British Virgins in late March.

Be sure to inform your charter company that you want to compete in one of these races, since some insurance policies exclude this sort of activity. In addition, racing sails generally are not available, although some charter companies will allow you to bring your own spinnaker.

An event strictly for luxury crewed yachts is the Chardonnay Classic, a series of straight-line races in the French Antilles. The series is hosted by Yacht Charters International in San Francisco.

See page 221 for more information on charter companies.

BAHAMAS AND NORTH AMERICA

BAHAMAS

The Bahamian chain of islands stretches from Bimini, just forty-five miles across the Gulf Stream from Miami, to the Turks, some 500-odd miles southwest. These 700 inhabited islands and 2,400 uninhabited cays stretch the length of Cuba and end just north of Hispaniola.

Unlike the Caribbean islands, which are really undersea peaks that rise out of deep water, the Bahamas is a shallow plateau with a few low-lying cays. Where the Caribbean islands are usually lush and verdant, the Bahamas are sparse and rocky, but it is the water that makes these islands so attractive. With almost no runoff from the islands to muddy the water, it remains almost transparent and, as you sail along, you can look down at the white-pink sand and watch rainbow-colored fish dart around the coral heads. You'll find more perfect sand beaches per mile in the Bahamas than anywhere.

One of the Bahamas is where Columbus actually discovered his "new world," making landfall in 1492 on San Salvador. Pirates and privateers preyed from the many cays on merchant ships returning from South or Central America laden with treasure. Eventually many of the islands were settled by American loyalists fleeing after the War of Independence, and many of their descendants are still there. In 1973, the Bahamas became an independent nation after three centuries as a British colony.

Today, the Bahamas rely heavily on tourist dollars, but charterers should be aware that the secluded cays and islets also have been used in recent years by drug smugglers who have shown little concern for lives or property. If you encounter suspicious activities, you should take extra precautions and probably find another anchorage. Be prepared to stop for inspections by Royal Bahamas Defence Force vessels as part of their battle against the smugglers.

Most chartering takes place in the Abacos and the Exumas, and there are major charter bases in both areas. Most of the Bahamas are served by airlines from the United States. Unless you particularly enjoy pushing a shopping cart, we'd recommend taking the provisioning package from the charter company for two reasons. First, supermarkets are as rare as mountains in the Bahamas and, second, the prices for food can be double (or more) the cost in the United States. Liquor, however, is cheap, with good rums about $5 per liter. In addition, there is often a 5 percent surcharge on credit card purchases. United States dollars are on a par with the Bahamian dollar, and are widely accepted.

It can be unnerving to sail with only a few feet of water under your keel but, after a day or two, you'll grow used to this "thin-water" cruising. Charts are generally reliable but, once you realize that nature has color-coded the shoals, you'll soon develop the ability to pick out the shallow spots. It's not hard to see the dark blotches of coral heads or rocks, and, as the sand bottom shoals, it changes from a washed-out blue to shades of white that signal the "uh-oh" areas.

While the Bahamian government has improved the navigational aids, bear in mind that this is not the United States. When a bulb burns out, it may not get replaced for weeks. We arrived once in a squally norther at Marsh Harbour and did not see the expected beacon. In between squalls, we used landmarks to follow the channel into the marina, but the dark sky made eyeball navigation nearly impossible. Later, having a calming drink, we found that some of the regulars in the bar overlooking the channel had placed bets on whether we'd make it, since the beacon had been turned off for several months!

When anchoring in some channels, the current can be quite

strong, so you'll want to learn the "Bahamas moor," which uses two anchors set as though they were to hold the bow and stern, but which are both led from the bow. This allows the boat to pivot around the bow to the current or breeze without swinging through the anchorage.

Weather: Most seasons are pleasant, although the hurricane season runs from July to November. Most charters take place in the winter months, but the months from January to April can bring an occasional norther that blows thirty-five knots or more and has heavy rain squalls. A norther usually blows itself out quickly, leaving settled weather and light breezes behind. Starting in June, the summer weather pattern brings light easterly winds with frequent calms, as well as uncomfortable heat and humidity.

The Abacos

Lying at the northeastern edge of the Bahamas bank, the Abacos are protected by a long barrier reef, with a string of small cays on one side and Great Abaco Island on the other to form the Sea of Abaco. Among the small cays are islands such as Man-O-War Cay, New Plymouth, and Hope Town, where the residents all seem to share the loyalist names of Albury, Lowe, and Russell. The villages are also reminiscent of Cape Cod, with narrow streets and waterfront clapboard buildings. Some of these islands remain nonalcoholic, and all have a strong Christian ethic, so bear that in mind as you cruise. Conch (pronounced "conk") is a staple in the local diet, and you'll be offered everything from conch burgers to conch fritters.

Because there are so many distractions, not to mention the many doglegs in the channels, allow extra time even though the straight-line distances are short. In a week you can probably take in the Sea of Abaco, seeing cays like those mentioned above plus Hope Town, Great Guana, and Treasure Cay, but you'd be better off taking more time.

Marsh Harbour is the center of Abaco action, but it only has one stoplight and two good markets near the dinghy dock. Nearby Hopetown has perhaps the most photographed lighthouse in the world with its candy-striped tower.

Man-O-War Cay has a reputation for boat building, and nearly everyone stops at "Uncle Norman" Albury's sail loft to buy souvenir duffel bags or canvas items.

Just north are Great Guana and Scotland Cays, both with outstanding snorkeling spots, and on the Atlantic side the beaches are equally spectacular. At Green Turtle Cay is New Plymouth, an English-style village with pastel-colored homes and the famous Blue Bee Bar at the south end of town. Its walls are papered with business cards of visiting sailors.

Grand Bahama and Bimini are usually not on the charterer's route because of their distance and their tendency to become congested with tourists and yachts from Florida.

The Exumas

Just over one hundred miles south of the Abacos are the Exumas, which are a spectacularly pretty cruising area. Eleuthera is also a good midpoint stopover for yachts sailing between the two island groups.

Mostly uninhabited, these cays create a smooth water buffer from the Atlantic. Highbourne Cay is usually the first stop, with provisions and evening calypso music as an enticement. At Allan's Cay, you can step back into prehistoric days as ancient iguanas lumber around hissing. Sampson's Cay is also appealing, and I can't think of Staniel Cay without my mouth watering for the tart key lime pie that's a specialty.

At Staniel, you can snorkel into nearby Thunderball Cave, where the James Bond film of the same name was shot. The cave has been compared to the Blue Grotto at Capri, although it has more sea life and better lighting. Go during slack water between the tides, because the current is strong. Georgetown, on Great Exuma, is another charter base, and has a number of good bays close by.

North America

The Florida Keys

The Keys conjure up images of Hemingway and Bogart, but these 800-plus islands are the only tropical cruising to be found in North America. Nicknamed "America's Out Islands" and stretching for 130 miles from Key Largo to Key West, the Keys allow you to select the level of adventure you want, with choices ranging from large marinas to deserted channels surrounded by mangroves.

While the weather, vegetation, and clear water are reminiscent of the Caribbean, there is an efficiency to cruising in your own country, with access to the Coast Guard, supermarkets, well-marked channels, and air-conditioned lodgings.

Charter companies operate in the Keys at Marathon as well as the Miami/Fort Lauderdale area and, depending upon your preferred style, you'll select from a wide variety of sail and powerboats. One caution, however: try to keep the draft of your charterboat under four feet or you'll be blocked from exploring some areas of the Keys.

Because the channels can be winding, narrow, and shallow, the Keys are not ideal for sailboat charters. On the other hand, you may wish to charter a small powerboat for zipping out on day trips, using the many air-conditioned resorts for your overnight bases.

One of the treasures of the Florida Keys is the coral reef that stretches the length of these islands. The third largest living reef in the world, it has been declared a national marine sanctuary to prevent damage to this incredible ecosystem. More than one million visitors come here to snorkel and dive, and boaters use mooring buoys instead of anchors to avoid damaging the reef.

The Intracoastal Waterway is usually calmer than Hawk Channel (which runs inside the coral reef but is otherwise open to the sea), and Plantation Yacht Harbor on Plantation Key has full facilities as well as a beach, which is a rarity in the Keys. The Intracoastal ends at Faro Blanco, whose harbor is marked by an old lighthouse. After that point, boats head outside to Hawk

Channel unless they're shallow enough to poke around through the Keys.

Key West, at the tip of the Keys, unfortunately has turned into a major tourist trap, but you can still find pleasure in the old clapboard houses. During the season, visitors are advised to radio ahead to reserve marina space since they fill up early.

If you have the time and inclination, heading offshore to explore the Marquesas Keys and the Dry Tortugas is worth the effort. The Marquesas are roughly twenty-five miles west of Key West, while the Dry Tortugas are another fifty miles west. Choose your weather with caution, however, since the seas can become nasty if the weather turns bad.

On the way to the Marquesas, be sure to watch your chart carefully and keep your eyes open to avoid running into coral heads when you near these islands. The harbor is just three feet deep, so larger boats need to anchor offshore.

The Dry Tortugas are remote enough that they are rarely crowded, and Garden Key has Fort Jefferson, which was built during the Civil War. A nearby underwater trail is a fun diversion, and the rangers who staff the island can tell you where the best dive sites are. Landing on Bush Key is prohibited because it is a wildlife sanctuary, but you can see huge numbers of birds here during the summer nesting season.

Weather: The best time to visit is from mid-January through May, although you can expect a few fronts to bring rain and cool weather. June to September is hot (90° F plus), humid, and buggy, but the fall months can be pleasant and uncrowded.

CHESAPEAKE BAY

For more than 200 miles from mouth to headwaters, the Chesapeake Bay is one of the great American charter areas. It is also the home port for an immense pleasure-boat fleet, so you'll often find traffic jams in the busier marinas. Less a bay than a huge semiprotected waterway, the more than 3,000 miles of shoreline are dotted with creeks and hidden anchorages, and the gently rolling scenery is not only beautiful but also filled with history at every turn. While the numbers are arguable, there are about 230 harbors and forty major rivers along the length of the Chesapeake.

A popular pastime is to explore the mazes of creeks and coves, but don't try to cover too much ground: local boaters have spent dozens of summers without seeing it all. Sit back, enjoy the farms and villages sliding past, and remember that you can always return for more.

Don't be surprised if you run aground, however, since it's standard procedure for every skipper in the bay. Go slowly when you're not sure of the depth and you can usually back off easily from the mud or sand bottom.

Annapolis, of course, is a major boating center, and on pleasant weekends the waters are literally covered with boats, including fleets of training boats from the Naval Academy. Nearby Spa Creek is secluded and snug, with overhanging willows and fine homes. The in-water boat shows in October make this a less desirable time to visit, since there are no guest slips or hotel rooms available during this period.

Across the bay, you can explore the beautiful Chester River lined with impressive plantation homes, and Chestertown's elegant red-brick Georgian buildings line the waterway.

St. Michael's on the Miles River has a superb maritime museum with guest moorings and a sleepy little town to explore, and you might see one of the famed Chesapeake log canoes out on the water with a tower of sail and the crew on hiking boards.

Tangier and Smith Islands provide a glimpse at fishing villages that haven't changed for a century, and the odd English dialect spoken here dates back to the late 1600s.

Weather: The cruising season, depending on how much cold you can stand, generally ranges from mid-April through October, but the locals say the spring and fall are the best, with settled conditions and gentle breezes. Midsummer brings light to non-existent winds, humidity, heat waves, violent thunderstorms, and invasions of jellyfish. Because the Chesapeake stretches inland, you can't count on a sea breeze to provide natural air conditioning. Early October is my favorite time, with the leaves beginning to turn, the flights of birds heading south, and the sun still warm at midday.

BAJA CALIFORNIA

Separated from the Pacific Ocean by the long arm of Baja California, the Sea of Cortez is one of the last great unspoiled cruising grounds. The beaches are still pristine and empty, the natives are friendly, and the sailing is marvelous. Until recently, the only way you could enjoy this area was to travel the 700-plus miles down from California on your own boat, which limited the cognoscenti to cruising sailors jumping off for the South Seas, or the idle rich. Charter services now make this cruising solitude as close and convenient as the nearest airport.

La Paz is the capital of Baja California, a city of 50,000 and mostly isolated from civilization except for the ferry to the Mexican mainland and jet flights from stateside. With complete provisions and full marine services available, this harbor is a popular yachting port of call as well as the base for the new charter service.

Scattered both north and south of La Paz along the eastern shore of Baja are dozens of largely uninhabited islands. Espíritu Santo shimmers invitingly in the heat haze just eighteen sea miles north of La Paz. Stretching eight miles in length, its craggy arms form a treasury of secluded coves and inlets, some with freshwater streams. Ashore, you might be treated to the sight of eagles feeding their young on a craggy volcanic cliff or find yourself being observed by timid desert animals. Rock hounds will delight in the geologic variety, and the truly indolent can contemplate a golden silence so pure it rings in the ears.

Snorkelers can scout the reefs or explore the famed oyster beds that once provided pearls for the crowns of Europe. The waters are swarming with fish, and even the most inept Izaac Walton might reel in a dorado or marlin.

Weather: November through May is the best cruising season, with warm days and soft nights. Be aware that in summer, both days and

The desert landscape of Baja California is stark, but the protected coves are plentiful and the water temperature is bathwater warm.

nights are hot, and fall can bring an occasional hurricane. A capricious local wind, the *coromuel,* can spring up suddenly, so stay alert.

SACRAMENTO DELTA

The California Delta is always a surprise to sailors unfamiliar with the area. San Francisco, just sixty-odd miles away, is renowned for the icy gales that blow through the Golden Gate, but the Delta is another world—one that Northern Californians use to balance out their rugged coastal waters.

Many visitors expect to see the undercivilized world and muddy backwaters of a Huck Finn story, but the sight of huge ocean-going freighters heading upriver, or the glimpse of a maxi-racer like *Kialoa* nestled behind an island quickly changes that impression.

With more than 1,000 miles of navigable waterways, the Delta is a vast network supplied by three rivers: the San Joaquin, Sacramento, and Mokelumne. Both Sacramento and Stockton are deep-water ports served by large ships, but it's the backwaters that attract the yachting crowd and that provide the basis for a booming houseboat charter business.

The Delta was once lowland marsh, but a vast reclamation project was started in the mid-1800s, using Chinese labor from the transcontinental railroad to build levees and turn river bottoms into fertile farmlands. Where paddlewheel steamers once carried mail and passengers, ski boats zip up and down the wide rivers, marlin-equipped sportfishers are tied to trees on the banks, and sailboats drift along in the gentle breezes. The mail is delivered by a postman in an outboard skiff, law and order is upheld by sheriffs in a flotilla of runabouts, and children use dinghies to catch the school bus.

Every area of the Delta has a personality of its own, and you can pick your spot by your mood. The Meadows, probably the best-known area, and Lost Slough both feature overhanging trees with branches trailing in the water, cool green glades, and silence that is almost overwhelming. Yet you're only a few minutes by runabout from several Delta hotspots where you can party late into the night. The settlement of Locke, built by and for the Chinese labor force, is almost a ghost town, with weathered clapboard buildings, creaky boardwalks, and fading paint marking a once-thriving playhouse.

If you want to keep moving, you can cruise along levees where, as in Holland, you're far above the farms as brightly colored crop dusters dart back and forth. If you'd rather sprawl in the cockpit with a cold beer and a lurid novel, you need only to find a convenient tree trunk and hitch up.

Weather: The climate is one of the drawing cards for the Delta, with hot summer afternoons and balmy evenings. Spring and fall are usually bright with cool evenings, while winter is pleasant, although the fog sometimes rivals London's best.

The Northeast

From mid-Connecticut to Maine, there is superb sailing in areas with such famous names as Cape Cod and Narragansett Bay, or among islands such as Block and Nantucket. Along the shore are sailing centers such as Mystic and Newport, and charter boats can be found in every harbor.

Weather: The season runs roughly from May through October for the Northeast, and the summer winds are generally reliable, although fog can sometimes be a problem for days at a time.

Maine

Maine is an area unto itself, known to old-timers as Down East (because it is downwind from Boston) and resembling Scandinavia in the rocky coves and islands found along the 200 miles of coastline. Although it has the same latitude as France, the Labrador Current sweeps past to ensure cold water year-round. When these waters meet the warm southwest winds, they turn Maine into a fog factory, with some areas averaging seventy-five foggy days a year.

Nevertheless, the beautiful scenery, sparse population, and crenellated coastline are an attraction for sailors. Only 250 miles in a straight line from border to border, the Maine coast is literally thousands of miles long when you include the coves, crannies, and more than three thousand islands (more than either French Polynesia or the Caribbean).

For the most part wild, rocky, and forested, the scenery is dotted with clapboard buildings and myriad lighthouses. Marinas outside the populated areas are few, but good anchorages are plentiful. Mount Desert is the largest of the many islands offshore, and the good harbors are often crowded in midsummer, although the creeks can often be empty.

Aside from the fog, navigation is straightforward, although you need to be prepared for up to twenty feet in tidal range, which can create fierce currents.

Weather: August is both the best cruising month and also the foggiest, and the short season lasts only from June through September.

Long Island Sound

Sometimes called the "Dead Sea" because of the notorious calms during the summer months, the sound is ninety miles long and twenty miles wide at the center. Because it is in the midst of the New York/Connecticut population center, this is an immensely popular sailing area in spite of the weather, which can be hot and humid in summer.

The entire shoreline is dotted with marinas, yacht clubs, and marine facilities, so it's quite possible to spend an entire summer simply hopping from one cove to the next. In fact, many Long Island sailors never take their boats offshore at all.

Great Lakes

The largest body of freshwater in the world, the Great Lakes are truly a huge inland sea that can generate their own weather system. The more than 8,000 miles of shoreline are often unspoiled, and several areas have become popular as charter-cruising sites. All of the Great Lakes can turn stormy with little notice, and sailors make listening to the weather forecasts a regular part of their routine. In addition, you need a little humility because the lake levels change every year, and the charts may be a bit off in the depths, which gives you the opportunity to bump occasionally.

Remember that the U.S./Canadian border wanders through these lakes, and if you cross into Canada, you need to be sure that you report to Canadian immigration and customs promptly at the nearest town. Pets must have vaccination certificates, and Canadian law prohibits drinking except in licensed dining rooms and bars, or in your home. You are allowed to drink aboard your boat ("home"), but only when it is tied up or anchored.

The North Channel is a roughly 120-by-20–mile segment of

Lake Huron along the Ontario shore of Canada and protected by Manitoulin Island from the lake itself. Most cruising sailors agreed that the 40-mile stretch from Killarney at the east to Detour Passage in the west is the best portion. Sometimes described as a state of mind, the North Channel is above all else quiet and serene. With rocky beaches and forested islands, the coves are often deserted and the sense of solitude is a delight, particularly when you are within a day's sail of large cities. The coves are often closely spaced, but rarely more than 20 miles from a town or village that can provide a pump-out station for your holding tank or a fresh supply of beer. Little Current on Manitoulin Island is the charter base for Discovery Yacht Charters, and has been called the "social center" of the North Channel. The storybook villages and spectacular rock formations, carved during the ice ages, are too numerous to mention and too numerous to include in a single charter, too.

The Apostle Islands at the western end of Lake Superior cover more than 1,000 square miles off the coastline of Wisconsin, with primitive landscapes and deep protected anchorages on twenty-two islands, twenty-one of which are inhabited only by deer, eagles, and loons. Known as the Apostle Islands National Lakeshore, the area features strange geologic formations worn by weather and glaciers, and hiking trails are found on most islands. Madeline Island has a quiet town much like a New England village. At the same latitude as Newfoundland, the water is chilly year-round.

Georgian Bay, on Lake Huron, has a multitude of rock-bound islands along the east shore, while cliffs and fjordlike channels mark the west.

Weather: In general, June through September is the peak charter and cruising season for the Great Lakes. July is the busiest month because of the long days and warmer waters; August has fewer mosquitoes, occasionally nippy evenings, and changeable weather. Normal wind patterns are westerlies that build in the afternoon before dying at night.

Southern California

Sprawling from Santa Barbara at the north to San Diego huddled against the Mexican border, Southern California has one of the largest boating populations in the world. Marina del Rey, with more than 6,000 boats, is the world's largest marina, and Newport Harbor is much like Newport on the East Coast with its expensive waterfront homes and old-money atmosphere.

In between are literally hundreds of marinas, which is somewhat of a surprise because cruising destinations (other than going to another marina) are somewhat limited.

Certainly the most popular destination is Catalina Island which, as the song says, is "twenty-six miles across the sea." Avalon is the only village on the island, but Two Harbors is a smaller outpost located at a narrow isthmus near the west end of the island. Many of the coves are privately leased to yacht clubs. Open anchorages in addition to the mooring buoys provided at Avalon and Two Harbors are available, although your chances of finding an empty buoy after breakfast on a summer Saturday aren't worth mentioning.

The Long Beach/Los Angeles Harbor, tucked behind a protective breakwater, is a minicruising area by itself. Farther south, Newport Harbor has Balboa Island in midchannel, and is literally wall-to-wall yachts, although transient moorings are available.

San Diego has an immense harbor that can take a day to sail to one end and back, and Mission Bay nearby is a huge man-made water playground with areas set aside for sailing, waterskiing, and swimming.

Weather: The boating season is year-round. The summer months are the most stable and the warmest. The westerly sea breeze is reliable, although an occasional Santa Ana, a hot offshore breeze, can whistle down the canyons in the fall, bringing sudden forty-knot blasts.

The harbor of Avalon, with the landmark Casino, is the most popular destination from the many marinas in Southern California.

PACIFIC NORTHWEST AND CANADA

Certainly the most popular charter area in the western United States is the San Juan Island chain, some sixty nautical miles north of Seattle. Charter boat fleets abound in Anacortes, which is just a few miles away on the mainland. If the San Juans are your cruising destination, try to pick up your boat nearby. Chartering a Seattle-based boat can cost you an entire day by the time you check out the boat, pass through two locks, and head north up Puget Sound—as well as another day at the end of the charter for the return trip.

With more than 200 rocky islands (750 if you count the small ones at low tide) and a dozen state parks left undisturbed, the forests and small villages are reminiscent of Maine. A good chartering area for beginners, the waters are reasonably protected even in storms off the Pacific. Friday Harbor, on San Juan Island, is the social and political center of the area, with a pleasant municipal marina and a one-street town lined with shops and restaurants. If you don't want that much civilization, you can leave the madding crowd behind and choose from the isolated outer islands, such as Stuart, with Reid and Prevost Harbors lying opposite each other, or Sucia Island, where Fossil Bay shows the Ice Age evolution of this island chain through embedded fossils and gouged rock. Roche Harbor, on the opposite side of San Juan Island, has a Victorian-era hotel where Teddy Roosevelt once stayed, and the marina has a flag-lowering ceremony every evening followed by a weather forecast that lists temperatures in other less fortunate cities across the nation.

Puget Sound, stretching for seventy-five miles from the tip of the Olympic Peninsula past Seattle and Tacoma to the myriad inlets and creeks at the southern end, is another popular cruising area also dotted with small towns, marinas, and anchorages.

North of the U.S./Canadian border are equally interesting charter areas, and the Gulf Islands are really a continuation of the San Juans under Canadian jurisdiction, although they tend to be more rocky than their southern kin.

Farther north, the Strait of Georgia forms an inland waterway under the protective bulk of Vancouver Island. Probably the most visited site for charterers is Princess Louisa Inlet, some forty miles up Jervis Inlet and past Malibu Rapids, where you have to wait for slack water to travel the tidal rapids. Once inside, however, the scenery is stunning, with 5,000-foot cliffs towering over the five-mile-long inlet, and Chatterbox Falls tumbling 120 feet down into the saltwater. Below the surface, the fjord is more than 1,000 feet deep. At dusk, you might see a bear strolling along the shore looking for dinner, and the smell of the pine forest lingers on the quiet air.

Given enough time, you can explore much of the coast of British Columbia, and Penmar Charters offers a yearly circumnavigation of Vancouver Island as a flotilla effort with crews joining and leaving at various points along the way.

You can even find charter activity in Alaska. Juneau is close to Glacier Bay National Park, the Tracy Arm-Fords Wilderness Area, and the Admiralty Island National Monument. A chain of high islands protects the Alaskan waterways, although the strong currents and large tidal range means this is an area for experienced skippers only.

Weather: Even in summer, the area is marked by rain and the winds are predominately light. The peak cruising season is the summer, from June through September, and the San Juans can be crowded from both visiting yachtsmen and tourists arriving by ferry. I prefer the "shoulder seasons" of May and early October when the islands are once again quiet and the weather is pleasant, although often nippy in the evenings.

Children play on rocks worn by the Ice Age in Sucia Island's Fossil Bay in the heart of the San Juan Islands.

EUROPE

For most Americans, chartering in Europe means the Mediterranean, that cauldron of ancient and modern culture that ranges from Spain's orange groves past the jet-set playgrounds of France, Monaco, and Italy to the birthplace of civilization, Greece. Included are seas with romantic names—Tyrrhenian, Ionian, Aegean, Adriatic—as well as a handful of major islands such as Malta, Sardinia, and Mallorca. New chartering areas are developing along the Turkish and Yugoslavian coasts, although at press time, civil unrest in the former Yugoslavia puts that area off limits.

The flip side of this sun-drenched Europe is the dramatic scenery and challenging sailing to be found in Northern Europe on the Baltic and North Seas as well as parts of the Atlantic. From Helsinki, Finland, on the east to the wild Hebrides of Scotland on the west, there is another world to explore with literally thousands of islands, the fjords of Scandinavia, and the lochs of Scotland providing grand landfalls and spectacular cruising.

GREECE

Certainly the most popular charter area in Europe (and thus worthy of a separate section), Greece brings Homer to mind. Though I've never seen his "wine dark seas," the shades of pale to dark blue are a stunning substitute. Everywhere you look, there are ancient ruins and history to absorb, as well as great natural beauty. The villages, sloping down to the tiny harbors like waterfalls of red-tile roofs and whitewash, are a contrast to the hillsides covered with olive trees, flashing silvery leaves in the sun. In the evenings, you can sit in your cockpit and listen to the soft sounds of bouzouki music drifting from the local *tavernas*.

Greece is a delight for charter sailors because the distances are relatively short between harbors, the navigation is purely by eye, and aside from the strong northeasterly *meltemi*, the weather is as stable as the Caribbean. The only real test for North American sailors is to learn how to "Med-moor" stern-to the quays, which can prove a challenge in a crowded harbor with a crosswind. But once settled in, the mooring is secure and doesn't require a dinghy to get ashore. Most crews pick up the technique easily.

The most popular cruising areas are the Saronic and Argolis gulfs, which are close to the charter bases at Piraeus as well as the

Many Greek harbors show the influence of a Moorish past, although the caiques at the quay are pure Greece.

gateway city of Athens. The popular islands of Aegina, Poros, Hydra, and Spetsai form a natural path leading to the Argolis Gulf. Because the distances are relatively short (twenty-five miles or less), there is time for leisurely sightseeing in the mornings before the breeze comes up, and in the afternoons after arriving in a new harbor.

The village of Perdica on Aegina is the first stop for most yachts since it is just fifteen miles from Piraeus (the seaport of Athens), and the island is noted for pistachio nuts, which you can buy fresh roasted from street vendors.

Poros, with more than 30,000 lemon trees, has great coves for a lunch stop and swim on the way to Hydra, which is a popular port for charterers. With the town built like an amphitheater on the slopes around the harbor, you can moor within feet of the outdoor *tavernas* that line the quay, but arrive early because the harbor fills up quickly.

Spetsai is forested with olive, cypress, and lemon trees that soften the rugged Greek terrain, and was featured in John Fowles's novel *The Magus*. No private automobiles are allowed on the island, and all transportation is either by taxi or horse-drawn carriage along streets lined with brilliantly white buildings.

The Sporades Islands on the eastern side of Greece are another popular area, with some of the prettiest islands in the entire Mediterranean. Often thickly wooded, the islands are a contrast to those in the Saronic Gulf. Skiathos (with its charter base), Skopelos (memorable for an attractive village rising steeply above the harbor), and Skyros, which has a fortified village, are the best known.

The Dodecanese Islands are Greek but closer to Turkey and similar in scenery. Kos is a charter base, dominated by a Crusader castle and known as the birthplace of Hippocrates, the father of modern medicine. Kalimnos is the sponge-fishing capital of the world, Leros has spectacular anchorages, and Patmos has the monastery of St. John looming over the whitewashed houses.

The Ionian Sea along the west coast of Greece has several charter bases for exploring a sea of islands. Levkas is blanketed with wild flowers in the spring, and there are dozens of pretty coves to explore, while Meganisi, Kalamas, and the mainland coast near Astakos are equally inviting. Of all the areas, however, the Ionian has the smallest number of ancient ruins.

At every island you can find wonderful food, including fresh tomatoes, olives, oranges, strawberries, and melons, plus the local yogurts, feta cheese, and fluffy pastries. No matter how well you stocked your charter boat, you'll end up buying fresh island bread just because of the smells wafting from the bakeries.

The Greek sense of time needs to be mentioned, since it is different from other European countries. Shops open early in the mornings and stay open late into the evening, but most residents take a lengthy midday nap. Dinner is served late; some restaurants don't begin serving until after 9:00 P.M. English is widely spoken, and both traveler's checks and major credit cards are generally accepted throughout the Greek islands.

Weather: The summers are hot and have strong *meltemi* winds from late June to early September. My favorite season is from mid-April to mid-May, when the temperatures range from 60° to 80° F, the winds are lighter but reliable, the crowds of tourists haven't arrived yet for the summer season, and mooring space is available. In the spring, the Aegean is still in bloom with flowers; the hills are green and water is plentiful. The after-summer season runs from mid-September to the end of October with similar conditions, but I've found that after the tourist crush of summer, the local citizenry is not as outgoing as they are in the spring.

SCANDINAVIA

From Finland on the east to Norway on the west, the whole of Scandinavia is a smorgasbord of delights, offering generally protected cruising grounds (especially in the areas where charter fleets are based), friendly people, often uncrowded anchorages, and a warmer and drier climate than Britain.

Mooring in Scandinavia differs from the Mediterranean practice of backing into the quay with a bow anchor out. Instead, northern sailors drop a stern anchor and then tie the bow to a tree or rock. You'll often see iron rings pounded into the rocks by the local sailing clubs for use on a first-come, first-served basis (unless marked private), and you'll know you've found a good anchorage.

Finland's biggest archipelago is off Turku in the southwest, with hundreds of islands in a fifty-mile arc. To the east in the Gulf of Bothnia are the Aland Islands where more than 6,500 islands lie between Finland and Sweden. Turku is a major base for charter companies, while Hango is a popular Finnish sailing resort. Because of the high latitude (most of the country is above 60° N, or higher than Anchorage, Alaska), the sailing season lasts from mid-June to mid-August. There is almost perpetual daylight during those months. Even in summer, the forested islands are usually deserted.

Sweden's "sun coast" is from Stockholm south about 120 miles along the Baltic sea coast roughly to Västervik, with sheltered sailing in the lee of the mainland. The Swedish coast has literally thousands of islands and three spectacular archipelagos. Starting at the north is the Stockholm archipelago, actually three distinct chains of islands with a reported 24,000 islets within an easy sail of the capital. Farther south are St. Anna's and Grynt, which offer an infinite choice of harbors and coves.

The islands are rocky remnants of the Ice Age glaciers, and Swedish sailors often moor by using a stern anchor and a line tied from the bow to shore. You can also "round moor," which involves swinging on a single anchor in midharbor. The Swedes respect privacy and solitude, so you'll find the anchorages quiet and fairly empty. Marinas are rare and there are few restaurants ashore, so plan to be self-sufficient once you leave the charter base. Liquor, by the way, is available only from state-owned stores, so stock up before you depart.

Navigation in Sweden (as in all of Scandinavia) is easy, with excellent charts and buoyage systems, but because the islands are gardens of rocks, it's easy to get disoriented. Keep track of your position on the chart or you'll wind up feeling as if you're lost in a maze. One pleasant attribute to the area is 0° of magnetic variation, which simplifies your chart work.

Denmark consists mostly of islands, and the waters are well

protected from North Sea storms. Distances are short between the many harbors and coves, so you can easily stop several times in a single day to explore. Denmark is lower and less mountainous than Sweden or Finland, and the island scenery consists of rolling hills and quaint villages.

The most popular cruising areas are the islands south of the main islands of Fyn and Sjaelland, and at the northern end of Jutland the waters of Limfjord, which connect the North Sea to the Kattegat. There are a multitude of marinas and yacht harbors, so many charterers choose to pick up moorings or transient docks every night, leaving their exploration of empty coves to the daytime. The Danish Yachting Association has mooring buoys (marked DS) in twenty-three harbors in Limfjord, and south of Fyn and Sjaelland, which can be used by visiting sailors for twenty-four hours with no charge.

Norway is probably the wildest of the Scandinavian cruising grounds, with deep fjords and sheltered islands. There are several charter bases on the southern and western coasts for both power and sailboats, and the rugged scenery is spectacular. There are few marinas, but every village has mooring space available for transient boats, whether they are fishing vessels or charter boats.

Weather: At 55° to 60° North, Scandinavia has short, brisk summers that last from May through September in Denmark and Sweden and June through August in Norway and Finland. The long days fade into a half-light from midnight to a 4:00 A.M. dawn in Finland and Norway, so you have plenty of time to sail in daylight. Temperatures can climb into the seventies during the days, although you'd be well advised to pack as many sweaters and jackets as you do bathing suits and shorts, because the conditions are changeable. Winds are generally light to moderate, although you can expect gusts near the valleys in Norway and Finland.

The British Isles

England, Wales, Scotland, and Ireland offer an almost endless variety of chartering possibilities, as well as something for every level of skill and pocketbook. Changeable weather, strong tidal currents, and rain are a part of the boating life throughout the British Isles.

Scotland

When I tell people that one of my favorite charter-cruising areas is Scotland, they always look at me oddly, as though white-sand beaches, balmy weather, and bathing suits are a prerequisite for any interesting sail.

Scotland is often windy and wet, but it is also picturesque and challenging sailing for the experienced crew. Although the country has many charter companies in both sail and power, few North Americans take advantage of this wild place.

The Hebrides, where Gaelic is the native tongue, provide spectacular Highlands scenery, with towering mountains and pristine villages on protected harbors. On the negative side, storms in the Atlantic Ocean are not a rarity, and the tides can be as high as nineteen feet in some areas. Currents sweep between the islands, so your navigation must be accurate, but you can find inside passages to most of the interesting areas. Oban is a popular charter base from which you can easily sail to the islands of Skye, Mull, Eigg, and Rhum. The main harbor of Skye is Portree, with a row of brightly painted houses lining the main quay, but there are numerous good anchorages on most of the islands. While the season generally ranges from late April to the end of September, the best time is in May and June, when the weather seems more settled.

One of my most memorable cruises took place inside Scotland when I chartered a powerboat on the Caledonian Canal, which cuts through the heart of Scotland in a chain of locks that connect the lochs, including the fabled Loch Ness. We didn't see "Nessie," but we did anchor in the lee of a ruined castle and locked right through the center of a town, where we could shop while waiting for the water to rise.

198 CHARTER AREAS

(Above) Sailing offshore in Scotland is challenging, since there are few good harbors like this one at Portree on the Isle of Skye.

(Below) Overlooking Loch Ness on Scotland's Caledonian Canal, the ruined Urquhart Castle is a popular stop for charterers exploring this area.

The English Channel

The most popular charter area in England is on the Solent, a twenty-mile stretch of the English Channel bounded by the Isle of Wight. From the hundreds of marinas in that area you can explore the creeks and harbors along the English coast, going as far as Devon and Cornwall, where the scenery is spectacular. You can also sail to France (Cherbourg is just sixty-five miles from the Isle of Wight) or, if you have more than a week, you can explore the Channel Islands.

Channel Islands

A part of the United Kingdom, although with their own parliament and tax system, the five major Channel Islands are just eighty-five miles from The Solent. This region is for experienced sailors only, since it has an extreme tidal range and currents as high as ten knots with over falls in the Race of Alderney area. This area is one of the most hazardous in Europe, with swirling currents, hidden rocks, and often changeable weather. The islands of Jersey and Guernsey are delightful, however, and the tiny island of Sark permits no cars but has three tiny harbors for access to the beautiful countryside.

The French coast of Brittany and Normandy is equally challenging. The harbors dry out at low tide, but the many islands, uncrowded beaches, and sunny climate have more in common with the Riviera than the rest of the English Channel.

Weather: English sailing is just what you might expect—a little of everything. Pack your sweaters and foul-weather gear along with your sunscreen, because even in midsummer, you can have both bright sun and pouring rain just hours apart. Good weather forecasts are available for the British Isles, and you should make a point of listening religiously.

Ireland

Another area often overlooked by North American charterers, Ireland has some superb sailing along the south and southwest coasts. The open-sea passages can test your skills and your stomach, but these are mercifully short and lie between protected sailing areas with good harbors.

Crosshaven is close to the international entry at Shannon, and the Royal Cork Yacht Club is the oldest in the world. From there you can sail as far as Bantry Bay, exploring harbors like Oysterhaven, with its emerald green hillsides, or Kinsale, a yachting center lined by beautiful Georgian homes. Castle Haven has a village with nearly vertical streets, and the beautiful harbor at Adrigold is protected by well-marked shoals. In between, you'll find numerous villages where you can stay in marinas while you sample the Guinness in the local pub, or you might choose secluded inlets (beware of those that dry out) for solitude. Charterers can even sail out to Fastnet Rock, but watch your weather—a sudden gale brought carnage to the experienced fleet in the 1979 Fastnet Race.

Weather: Irish weather is temperamental. Although the Gulf Stream flows along the coast, the water is cold even in midsummer, and the air temperature rarely reaches 80° F even during the season from May through September.

Northern Europe

While the Mediterranean coast of France is the most famous, the best sailing is certainly along the Brittany coast, which also has a number of charter bases. Morbihan (Breton for little sea) has fifty mostly uninhabited islands with white-sand beaches, good anchorages, and a warm, sunny climate. There are creeks and villages to explore, as well as some lovely old towns like Vannes, with its thirteenth-century cathedral, and Aurray with its gabled houses. (Again, be prepared for an extreme tidal range as well as riverlike currents.) You can even sail up the River Vilaine to the city of

Redon, passing wonderful creeks for overnight mooring as well as towns and villages to explore.

The Netherlands is more water than land, and most of it is reclaimed from the sea by technology and tenacity. The Ijsselmeer (pronounced *ice-el-mir*) was created in 1932 when the Zuiderzee was cut off from the North Sea by massive dikes. Fed by rivers, it is now the largest freshwater lake in Europe as well as a popular charter cruising area. With steady 15- to 20-knot breezes and short distances between the marinas and villages, it is a pleasant area for novices and experts alike.

Volendam is touristy but pretty, with colorful houses along the water, while Muiden has an excellent marina and a massive castle, Muiderslot, that dates to 1280. Hoorn is a charming shipping town, and Makkum is notable for its pottery that uses more colors than the traditional Delft blue. Sail up the Amstel River to the edge of Amsterdam if you want a taste of cosmopolitan life.

Aside from the Ijsselmeer, the Wadden Zee is a less-populated area on the North Sea coast, and Zeeland is an area of islands and inlets bordering Belgium.

Weather: Throughout most of Northern Europe, the sailing season runs from May through September. The climate is temperate, with temperatures rarely exceeding 65° F in summer, and rainfall is frequent year-round.

MEDITERRANEAN

Stretching 2,300 miles from Gilbraltar to the shores of Lebanon and Israel, the Med is a vast and tideless sea, warmed by the hot lands of North Africa and by the southern shores of Europe. The North African and Middle Eastern coast is generally inhospitable, both in cruising facilities and because of the general civil unrest that affects the region.

The northern shore, however, provides some superb cruising for charterers. The Spanish coast is undeveloped for chartering, but everything changes at the French border. The Riviera has two faces, with low hills and sandy beaches from Cap Roux to Nice, and the distinctive reddish mountains from Nice to the Italian border, with cliffs to the water's edge and numerous harbors.

A number of charter companies operate along the Riviera, but this type of chartering caters to those who prefer their pleasures ashore rather than at sea. With light breezes throughout the summer, most charterers simply cruise from port to port, mooring Med-style and going ashore to sample the gastronomic and shopping pleasures of ports such as St. Tropez, Antibes, Cannes, and Portofino.

Corsica, lying south of Genoa, is nevertheless French and quite beautiful, with 9,000-foot mountains, palm-lined beaches, and ancient buildings. The water is clear and warm, with good sailing breezes, although you need to watch for navigation hazards like underwater rocks. The island has several charter companies, some of which have two bases for one-way charters, and it's an easy

St. Tropez certainly is the best-known destination on the French Riviera, with cafés along the quay to lure crews from the Med-moored yachts.

Porto Cervo, the heart of jet-set Costa Smeralda on the Italian island of Sardinia, attracts fleets of chartered mega-yachts as well as smaller charter boats at the piers.

---

sail to the Costa Smeralda jet-set playgrounds on Sardinia or to Elba, which has many lovely coves and anchorages.

Weather: The cruising season for the Riviera is long by most charter standards, ranging from April through the end of October, but I would avoid August since most of Europe takes its vacation at that time. In fact, summer tourist traffic in towns like Portofino can be so heavy that it takes several hours to travel a single mile, so be wary of June through August in general.

Turkey

At the eastern end of the Med lies Turkey, which is a relatively recent addition to the charter world. The pine-covered mountains and occasional waterfalls are a pleasant change from the dry and rocky islands in the Med, but the turquoise seas and sheltered bays are the real drawing cards.

The Aegean coast and the Mediterranean shores are the most popular, since the Black Sea along northern Turkey has many restricted areas. The western and southern coastlines are dotted by a multitude of pretty bays, beaches, and harbors, as well as incredible historical and archaeological sites worthy of exploration.

The foods of Turkey blend the cuisines of Asia and Europe with shish kebabs, incredible fresh vegetables, and good wines. Be wary of raki, an aniseed aperitif known locally as "lion's milk" with good reason. Carpet shops are found under awnings, and you can barter for your Persian rug over a cup of tea in a most civilized manner. Provisions and water are generally available, marinas are found in the larger cities, and the fresh-produce markets are exceptional throughout Turkey.

Bodrum is a charter base as well as the yachting capital of Asia Minor, and has a magnificent Knights of Rhodes fortress dating to the 1400s. The other charter base of Marmaris (not to be confused with the Sea of Marmara), just thirty miles from Rhodes, has a sixteenth-century fortress overlooking the city. Between Marmaris and Antalya are a number of delights: the ruins and long beach of Xanthus, the port towns of Kas and Kalkan, Kekova's dozens of islets and a sunken Lycian city to snorkel, and Antalya, close to the great sites of Perge and Side. Fethiye, near the southern tip, lies on a bay filled with lovely islands and gleaming white-sand beaches below the rock tombs of former kings.

Weather: Turkish summers are hot (July and August temperatures are as high as 100° F) and crowded. The Aegean shore is affected by the *meltemi* winds from May through September, while the southern coastline has light breezes and calm nights. Thunderstorms are most frequent in spring and autumn. In general, the cruising season lasts from early April through October; experienced charterers tend to prefer October.

SOUTH PACIFIC AND ASIA

*A*fter Nordhoff and Hall wrote of *Bounty*'s landfall at Tahiti, generations of armchair sailors have dreamed of the scent of the South Pacific. The jumbo jet and the charter yacht have brought this area within reach of every sailor longing to smell the frangipani on a warm tradewind.

Tahiti

Known officially as the Society Islands, this French archipelago lies halfway between Australia and California, and the primary charter grounds are the Leeward Islands (Îles sous le Vent) at the northern end of the island chain. For most armchair cruisers, the names of Bora Bora, Huahiné, and Raiatéa conjure up images of coco palms swaying over clear blue water and jagged volcanic peaks soaring into vivid South Pacific sunsets. Best of all, it's true. The Society Islands of French Polynesia are the stuff of dreams.

Four major islands comprise the chartering area: Raiatéa, Tahaa, Bora Bora, and Huahiné. While Tahaa and Raiatéa share the same boundary reef, the other two islands are roughly a half day's sail away. Once inside the protective reefs (entrances are well marked), you can sail for hours in the smooth waters past the jagged volcanic mountains and lush green valleys. Anchorages are plentiful on the islands themselves as well as on the *motus,* tiny islets on the barrier reef. There's no shortage of either lunch stops for swimming on the white-sand beaches or protected harbors for stress-free overnight mooring.

On a seven-day charter, you'll have to make some tough decisions about itinerary, since there is too much to see in such a short time. Bora Bora is a must, if only to sail through the pass and see the magnificent peaks wreathed in clouds. Huahiné, particularly the southern end, is unspoiled, as are the southern and northern areas of both Raiatéa and Tahaa.

Raiatéa alone is enough for a week's vacation, and some charterers never depart from the Raiatéa/Tahaa reef, spending their days exploring the numerous deep fjords and the *motus.* Uturoa, the main town in the Leewards, offers a taste of French Polynesia without the jaded and grimy feel of Papeete, the capital and main city of Tahiti, which tends to be overrun by tourists. By contrast, Uturoa has friendly people and a leisurely pace still unaffected by the dozens of jumbo jets that now descend into Tahiti. Uturoa also has an incredible fresh-produce market and the volcanic soil produces superb fruit, including a sweet pineapple not to be missed.

Bora Bora, with two extinct volcanoes rising from a cobalt sea, is one of the world's most recognizable landfalls and was the inspiration for the mythical Bali Hai in *South Pacific.* Because of that attraction, it is dotted with tourist hotels and is a typical Club Med playground, but you can still find pleasant anchorages and superb snorkeling away from the shoreside disco atmosphere. Be sure to get a radio check on the single pass through the reef before heading for Bora Bora, however, because it is sometimes closed by breaking seas.

Raiatéa is the charter base for The Moorings and ATM Yachts, and is known as the "sacred one" to Polynesians. You won't be the only ones to set sail from this largest island in the Leeward Chain, though: every great Polynesian sea voyage began from a *marae,* or temple, at Opoa on this island, including the migrations to Hawaii and New Zealand.

Huahiné is the garden island, steadfastly cultivating crops

instead of tourists, so it remains much as Captain Cook might have seen it. The usual first stop on Huahiné is off the village of Fare, but the lagoon at Baie d'Avea at the south end of the island is also an attractive anchorage with a good sand bottom and an astounding reef filled with brilliantly colored and fearless tropical fish. (When packing for the charter, include a bottle of hydrogen peroxide or Betadine antiseptic to treat any coral cuts, which can quickly become infected otherwise.) Port Bourayne at midisland is startlingly similar to a Scottish loch.

From Huahiné, you can sail to Tahaa for lunch at the Hibiscus Hotel, where you'll be greeted by the immense pet pig, Lala. The *motus* at the north end of Tahaa provide good anchorages, and Motu Diego has the François restaurant, which serves authentic, expensive gourmet food at a bungalow-getaway owned by a French/Swiss couple.

While the trips between the major islands involve open-sea crossings, the steady 15- to 20-knot tradewinds provide reasonably predictable breezes for much of the year. You need to remember that all of Polynesia uses the European IALA-A buoyage system with red to port (red-to-red returning). Inside the reefs, a hybrid system marks the lagoons by land or reef side, but all buoys are well maintained. Navigation is "sail by colors": dark-blue water is deep, light blue or brown is thin, and white (either transparent or foamy) water being never-never land where birds stand. All of the charter boats are equipped with anchor windlasses, a necessity for anchoring in water as deep as one hundred feet in the island fjords. Because navigating at night is dangerous, the charter companies suggest that you be anchored by 5:30 P.M. and leave for other islands before 9:30 A.M. to make sure you arrive early.

French Polynesia has acquired a well-deserved reputation for being expensive, so you should plan to dine aboard regularly and save restaurants for special occasions. A bottle of Hinano, a local beer, costs $3–$4 at a bar, a decent French wine costs $12–$16 at a restaurant, and a hamburger with french fries can cost $10. Be sure to bring enough sunscreen, film, and other necessities, because they are pricey ashore. On the other hand, it's hard to leave

Off the shore of Tahaa in French Polynesia, this crew sails in company with a school of dolphins who love to play in the bow wave of charter yachts.

a village without a baguette of French bread (the smell wafts from the bakeries), a plastic jug of pleasant *vin ordinaire,* or a cone of homemade coconut ice cream.

Chartering in the Leewards is almost more accessible than the Caribbean, particularly from the West Coast: the nonstop flights take just eight hours, and Raiatéa is a quick forty-five-minute shuttle further. It's best to visit soon, however, because several hotels are under construction and some travelers fear that the Leeward Islands will soon become "Waikiki South."

Weather: The charter high season runs from June through September. This is winter below the equator, when the trade winds blow steadily from the southeast. The months from November through April are the wet season, with high humidity, occasional rain, warm temperatures, and light breezes. The dry season is from May through October, with lower humidity and steady tradewinds.

Temperatures average 79° F, ranging from the 90s in the wet season to the mid-80s in the dry.

New Zealand

New Zealand provides spectacular chartering opportunities, and it's no surprise that the country has more boats per capita than any other nation.

The Bay of Islands, certainly the most popular destination for both locals and foreign sailors, is located at the eastern tip of North Island, known locally as Northland. At 35° S, the area has a mild subtropical climate, and this protected bay holds literally hundreds of uninhabited islands. Within a forty-five-mile stretch of coastline, there are eighty-six islands and a handful of charter companies that serve the area. Opua and Russell are the two main charter bases, and both are set nearly in the center of a cruising area that extends from the village of KeriKeri in the west to Cape Brett at the east, although longer charters sometimes explore outside those boundaries. The scenery is delightful, with fertile green pastures rolling down to white beaches edged by emerald water that is clear enough to check your anchor.

The Bay of Islands Maritime and Historic Park is a preserve that keeps the islands in a pristine state, and local sailors take pride in the spotless conditions. A garbage barge is provided at the southeast end of Motorua during the summer season, and at the southwest end of this same island, a buoy holds a water hose from a freshwater stream for the free use of cruising sailors. Motorua also has nature trails marked for flora and fauna, and you can stroll through the stands of pine and plunge into a cool tropical forest filled with giant ponga ferns. Pipi Bay is named after the clamlike bivalves that are found a few inches below the surface of the sand (look for tiny air bubbles) and then steamed and dipped in a garlic-butter broth. Throughout the islands, the diving and snorkeling are superb.

Te Hue Bay is sheltered and has a superb beach reached by crossing a spit of land. (The name means Assassination Cove—the

New Zealand's Bay of Islands provides cruising through a protected island chain, as well as opportunities for hiking and exploring ashore. (Photo courtesy Rainbow Yacht Charters)

Maoris massacred early French explorers for violating their sacred areas.) World cruiser and naturalized New Zealander Eric Hiscock called Opunga Cove his favorite. On Motuarohia is a plaque commemorating Captain Cook's first explorations of the area, and the anchorages are overlooked by an ancient Maori fortress. Otehei Bay is another good anchorage that is well protected from the easterly winds that come with rain, but it is often crowded.

At the east end of the bay is Cape Brett, where sailors often encounter large swells rolling in from the South Pacific. If the weather is calm, however, you can sail around the point and south to Whangamamumu Harbor, the site of an ancient whaling station. Above the pond is a lovely freshwater waterfall that local sailors use as a natural shower and laundry.

At the western end of the bay is KeriKeri, a delightful village noted for citrus products. On the way into the long cove are several lovely bays, the best of which is Opito. Once at KeriKeri you need to watch the tides, but you can enjoy the pubs, shops, and local residents. KeriKeri Radio produces a useful chart showing all the good anchorages and marine facilities in the Bay of Islands. If you don't get one with your boat, you can pick it up at most shops or chandleries.

At Russell is a Park Visitor's Center, which has a worthwhile audio-visual presentation about the islands, as well as waterside taverns that retain the flavor of the region's wild whaling days.

While the Bay of Islands has reaped most of the publicity for chartering, the Hauraki Gulf near Auckland is the country's most active sailing area, and also the location of several charter companies. As the water gateway to Auckland, the entire area is part of the Hauraki Gulf Maritime Park. There are dozens of lovely anchorages both north and south of Auckland, as well as an array of islands, many uninhabited, and pretty beaches. The scenery is varied, ranging from rugged cliffs to rolling pastures and forests, and the entire Gulf is well protected from all conditions except northers.

Across the Hauraki Gulf is the Coromandel Peninsula. The city of the same name was once a gold-rush boom town but is now a quiet village surrounded by abandoned mines. Nearby Te Kouma Harbour is a better protected overnight anchorage. Port Fitzroy on nearby Great Barrier Island is a delight, with numerous smaller bays that offer either solitude or quaint villages where you can dine on mussels and Steinlager.

The largest island is Waiheke, roughly ten miles east of Auckland. It has good protection from the prevailing southwesterlies in anchorages such as Omaru, Little Muddy, and Man O'War Bay.

One company, Rainbow Charters, offers a twenty-one-day one-way bareboat charter from Auckland to the Bay of Islands (or back), which takes you off the tourist path to explore the northeast coast and its secluded anchorages, islands, and wildlife sanctuaries.

Both the Bay of Islands and the Hauraki Gulf are well charted with few hazards, and both have a well-maintained European buoyage system.

Protected anchorages are a trademark of New Zealand's Bay of Islands. (Photo courtesy Rainbow Yacht Charters)

Weather: The best sailing season is from the end of October through mid-May during the southern spring, summer, and fall. Most New Zealanders do their cruising from December through February, so the anchorages are busier in those months when the daytime temperatures are in the mid-80s and the breezes are in the ten- to fifteen-knot range. The New Zealand winter, from June through September, has cooler temperatures and stronger winds.

Tonga

Just 1,000 miles from New Zealand (not far by South Pacific standards), Tonga is a land that time forgot, although it is called "the land where time begins" because it lies on the international dateline. Tonga also lives up to the nickname "The Friendly Islands," applied when Captain James Cook first visited this gorgeous region in the late 1700s. Time does seem to stand still here, and life proceeds at a sedate pace.

The last of the Polynesian kingdoms, Tonga has the longest unbroken monarchy in the world. Lying between 15° and 23.5° South, Tonga consists of three distinct archipelagoes. Vava'u, the northernmost chain, is the charter area. A string of islands and reefs that shelter the islands from the wind and seas of the open Pacific makes the Vava'u group essentially an island-studded lake, with conditions similar to those in the Virgin Islands. The breezes are steady tradewinds that sweep the Pacific, and the water is warm and remarkably clear.

Best of all, there are more than fifty anchorages that one charter company terms "world class," and all are spectacularly beautiful and close together, so you can explore several in a day.

Because Tonga has remained off the beaten path for so many centuries, it hasn't been Westernized, and the Tongans remain proud, gracious, and gentle. Tipping is not permitted. The Sabbath remains a day of rest, and Tongans do not swim, fish, play games, or work on Sunday. In fact, a check signed on a Sunday is not valid. By the same token, the dress code ashore remains conservative: men are expected to wear shirts in public, while women should leave their bikinis to the privacy of the boat or an uninhabited islet.

Neiafu is the biggest town in the Vava'u chain, and the base of charter operations. The eastern islands are low and surrounded by the protective reefs, while the western islands are volcanic remains that rise from deep water. Maninita is as far south as most charterers venture, but it is a hauntingly beautiful island where you can anchor off a talcum-soft beach and row ashore. The big-leafed puleo trees turn the interior into a cool, green glade that silences even the noise of the surf, and you can easily walk across to the ocean beaches on the opposite side.

Hunga Lagoon is nearly landlocked, and you can sail west from Hunga if you want to try your hand at deep-sea game fishing for tuna, dorado, and the occasional sailfish, but be sure to request fishing gear from the charter company. Just south is Foeata, a pleasant lunch anchorage with excellent snorkeling, like Mounu.

One surprise to charterers are the sea caves of Tonga, which are ideal for exploring. Swallows Cave is on the northern tip of Kapa Island, and you should row into it in the late afternoon to get the best lighting on the incredible colors. Mariner's Cave is located at the northwestern end of Nuapapu Island and requires visitors to dive through an underwater entrance, surfacing in another grotto filled with turquoise light. As with Swallows, the best time to go is the late afternoon.

Plan to dine on board, since the only real restaurants are at the starting and ending point of Neiafu—although you may find that a Tongan feast has been arranged by the charter company at one of the islands. This is likely to include Tonga delicacies such as lobster, pork, fish, papaya, bananas, coconuts, and yams, a Tongan staple. More important, the Tongans are genuinely friendly, and their enthusiasm for song and dance is contagious.

Weather: Remember that Tonga is below the equator, so the seasons are reversed. The coolest weather (and the shortest days) are in July and August, when the temperatures average 65° to 75° F. For most of the year, however, you can expect midday highs in the 80s and lows in the 70s. Hurricane season is from January through March, but storms generally are forecast well in advance. Because the months of June through August are the southern winter, the charter companies are often busy with bookings from Australians getting away to a warm climate, and the prime charter season spans from April through November.

AUSTRALIA

A land mass the size of the continental United States, Australia has a number of charter opportunities, but two areas in particular seem to draw both the locals and the foreigners time after time.

The Whitsundays off the Queensland coast are a chain of ninety-seven islands so named by the ubiquitous Captain Cook aboard *Endeavour* in 1770 because he arrived on Whitsunday. Rocky but forested with pine and eucalyptus, they are protected from the ocean swells by the Great Barrier Reef and, as Cook noted, the area is "one continued safe harbour." Literally an inland sea behind the protective Great Barrier Reef, the area has hundreds of lovely anchorages and beaches within short sails of one another, and the area has been called a "Down Under Virgin Islands" for the pleasant conditions.

Shute Harbour and Airlie Beach on the mainland are the starting point for many charters (although companies also are based at Pioneer Bay, Abel Point, and at Hamilton Island) because it lies within a fifteen-mile radius of the heart of the best cruising area. Except for a handful of resorts, the islands have been maintained in a natural state as a national park, and the only improvements are a few barbecue pits, trash barrels, and moorings.

It would take several weeks even to superficially explore most of the islands, and charterers uniformly complain that they didn't have enough time. The best advice from local sailors is simply to relax, enjoy four or five good anchorages during a one-week charter, and come back another time for the rest.

Most charterers head for Palm Bay or Happy Bay after they check out the boats and stow their gear, since these good anchorages are just an hour's sail from Shute. Both have moorings provided by the local resorts so you don't have to worry about anchoring on the first night.

Nara Inlet, a steep-walled slash into Hook Island, is said to be the best anchorage in the Whitsundays (watch for the cockatoos in the trees), and the island also has the highest peak at 1,478 feet. Herds of goats once roamed the island, placed there to help shipwrecked sailors survive, but today visitors find the 8,000-year-old Aborigine cave paintings more interesting.

The north side of Hook is a seemingly endless string of bays with perfect coral reefs for diving and snorkeling, and Butterfly Bay is one of the best. Watch for coral heads on the entry, then row to the head of the bay where the creek leads to a rocky pool of freshwater shaded by trees that are often filled with butterflies.

Whitsunday Island, the largest island in the chain, has Whitehaven Beach at the east end. This is a three-mile stretch of squeaky white sand that is 99 percent silica instead of the usual beach of fine coral fragments. Bareboat charters aren't allowed to explore the Great Barrier Reef, but floatplanes land at Whitehaven Beach to pick up anyone who wants to fly across for a couple of hours of snorkeling or reef-walking. Several bays on the south side of Whitsunday Island, such as Turtle Bay, also have excellent coral reefs, but these are not suitable for overnight mooring when the tradewinds are blowing.

If civilization appeals to you, radio ahead for a marina berth at Hamilton Island, the largest island development on the Australian coast. With its high-rise resort, jet airport, and bustling atmosphere of restaurants and bars, it's a startling counterpoint to the otherwise untouched Whitsundays.

Be aware of the tides in the Whitsundays, since some of the narrow passages between islands can become maelstroms when a five- to six-knot current runs opposite the wind. Tidal range averages twelve feet, although it can reach eighteen feet during spring tides, so anchor accordingly. You'll also need to plan ahead at some inlets, where the water may shoal when the tide drops ten or twelve feet. Be prepared for "bullets," the Aussie term for blasts of wind funneled down the mountain slopes and seemingly aimed directly at you when you're trying to set your anchor.

Australian regulations limit the maximum number of people aboard a bareboat charter yacht to eight, regardless of the number of berths the yacht may have. Anchoring is important because of the currents and tradewinds, so hone your skills before you set sail. As an added safety factor, all charterers are required to check in daily by VHF. Navigation is straightforward, the islands are well charted, and the clear water makes eyeball navigation easy. Don't forget to look at the night sky, where you'll see the Southern Cross.

Weather: Lying about 20° South, the Whitsundays are balmy in winter and hot in summer. The charter season is from May through October, although chartering is permitted year-round. The windiest months are April to August when the southeast tradewinds blow steadily, and the rainy months are January to March, when there is also the chance of cyclones. December through April are the summer months, but September is less crowded and recommended by locals. Water temperatures range from 79° F in April to 72° F in July.

Almost within sight of Sydney is a second charter area that is popular with Australians but overlooked by most overseas visitors. The Pittwater/Hawkesbury waterways are not far from Sydney's northern limits, but the timber-covered hills and spectacular sandstone cliffs (and their status as a national park) have resisted all development.

This is powerboat charter country with three national parks to cruise through, including what Australians call a "foreshore" with the Hawkesbury River feeding an immense estuary. Many areas have guest moorings, a necessity because of the often deep water. The Pittwater arm of this cruising area has Scotland Island at the south end, and beaches along the eastern shore.

The Hawkesbury River leads more than fifty miles inland, winding through high cliffs, forests, pleasant villages, and uninhabited islands. Cowan Water, which lies west of the Hawkesbury River, has a handful of coves with moorings and even a waterfall. All of this is just half an hour from downtown Sydney by commuter train, and a handful of charter companies offer powerboats of all shapes and sizes.

THAILAND

If I had to choose one area as the newest charter "hot spot" it would be Thailand, which defines the word "foreign" for most visitors. On the way to your charter base, you might drive by Jeep through cool green rubber plantations, past golden Buddhist temples, around water buffalo lounging in the road, and along some of the most incredibly beautiful coastline in the world. Once called Siam and the setting for *The King and I,* Thailand is a new addition to the international charter world.

Most of the country's perfect sand beaches are not only uncrowded, but also devoid of the human contamination found elsewhere in a world filled with beer bottles and Styrofoam. The rock formations found in Phang Nga Bay defy description. Thailand has been compared to the Caribbean of Hemingway's time: untouched and absolutely enticing. When you anchor, you can look down through sixty feet of water and clearly see the shackle on your anchor. Local fishermen offer to share their catches of fish and lobster with visitors, and often are embarrassed at the offer of a few cans of cola in exchange for the pet-sized lobsters.

Thailand is not as close as the Caribbean to North America, of course, which has served to dissuade all but a few crewed charter yachts from venturing into these waters. Recently, however, both European and American bareboat charter companies have set up bases here.

Located in the Andaman Sea at the southern end of the Thai peninsula leading to Malaysia, the island of Phuket (pronounced

This strange rock formation is near James Bond Island in Thailand's Phang Nga Bay, where the 007 film Man with the Golden Gun *was filmed.*

poo-ket) is a growing Asian tourist resort with the usual beachfront condos, tourist shops, noisy motorbikes, and late-night discos. But the offshore regions, with a few exceptions, have been left undiscovered except by local fishermen and a few cruising sailors passing through the area.

Phang Nga (pronounced *fang-naw*) Bay east of Phuket is an eerie place with hundreds of huge limestone pillar islands that rise sheer from the surface of the sea. In midbay, these bizarre geologic monuments rise in every direction, fading into the haze like an Asian watercolor painting. The setting for the 007 film *Man with the Golden Gun,* James Bond Island is usually overrun by tourist boats, but the rest of the bay remains untouched and protected. These towering islands are notched with caves in which the Thai people collect swallows' nests, using rickety bamboo scaffoldings, for bird's nest soup.

Deep water surrounds these islands and charts are good, so you can explore the area to your heart's content. You might even find some of the "hollow" islands where caves lead into silent inner lagoons. At the north end of the bay is Ko Pan Yia, a Muslim settlement with its own mosque, shops, and restaurants, all on stilts over the water. Farther south you'll encounter the "sea gypsies" at Chao Lai, who live off the sea aboard their boats.

The Similan Islands, fifty miles west of Phuket in the Andaman Sea, are a chain of nine large and small government-protected gems with lush forests and rounded boulders reminiscent of those at The Baths in Virgin Gorda. The brilliant tropical fish seem to know they are protected, as they swim right up to peer into snorkelers' face masks, and the soft white-sand beaches are empty.

On a recent crewed powerboat charter in Thailand, I found myself sitting every evening in the cockpit as blue-white slashes of lightning flashed across the distant skies over the mountains. During the afternoons, towering pillars of cumulonimbus clouds had grown into crennelated towers above the overheated mainland. After dark, the air was still and balmy in our quiet anchorages, and the only sound was the wavelets shushing onto the white-sand beach. It was a spectacular light show.

In addition to the Similan Islands, there are another three

dozen islands scattered along the Thai coast. The Phi Phi Islands to the southeast have teeming marine life that attracts scuba divers. To the north, the islands of Koh Surin are equally idyllic. Ko Racha Yai, just south of Phuket, has a marvelous deep cove with water so still that it reflects millions of tropical stars.

Just as spectacular as the scenery in Thailand is the absence of other yachts. In fact, on my last charter in Thailand, we did not see any other boat for four days.

Ashore, Thai cuisine combines seafood, meat, and vegetables with coconut milk, lime, hot chilis, and an array of spices into meals that are unique in the world. Be wary of green curries, however, unless you have a leatherlike palate. Local restaurants often don't bother with menus, and simply serve what was caught live that afternoon.

Racers can get into the action in Thailand during the sixty-mile Andaman Sea Race from Phi Phi to Phuket in early December, or the King's Cup series of buoy races in mid-December.

Weather: The prime season for Phuket and the Andaman Sea runs roughly from November through April, when the northeast breezes blow steadily, the humidity is relatively low, and there is virtually no rain. For the Gulf of Thailand, the season runs from January through August. The summer monsoon season, with daily rain and high humidity, lasts from June through October, and midsummer months have a threat of typhoons. Temperatures range from 80° to 90° F year-round.

CHARTER COMPANIES

*T*he initial listings are international charter companies with multiple bases worldwide. Contact them for information on their various locations and boat types. The remaining companies are listed according to their charter base locations.

The Moorings
19345 U.S. Highway 19N,
#402
Clearwater, Florida 34624
(800) 535-7289

Privilege Charters
1650 S.E. 17th Street, #204
Fort Lauderdale, Florida
33316
(800) 262-0308

Sunsail
2 Prospect Park
3347 N.W. 55th Street
Fort Lauderdale, Florida
33309
(800) 327-2276

ATM Yacht Charters
3471 Via Lido #206
Newport Beach, California
92663
(800) 227-5317

NorthSouth Yacht Vacations
655 Dixon Road, Suite 18
Toronto, Ontario M9W 1J4
Canada
(800) 387-4964

VIRGIN ISLANDS

Avery's Marine
P.O. Box 54248
St. Thomas, United States
Virgin Islands 00803
(809) 776-0113

Charter Companies

Bitter End Yacht Club (Virgin Gorda)
875 N. Michigan Avenue #3707
Chicago, Illinois 60611
(800) 872-2392

Caribbean Adventures
Box 9997
Yacht Haven Marina
St. Thomas, United States Virgin Islands 00801
(800) 626-4517

Caribbean Sailing Charters
3883 Andrews Crossing
Roswell, Georgia 30075
(800) 824-1331

Caribbean Yacht Charters
Box 583
Marblehead, Massachusetts 01945
(800) 225-2520

Caribbean Yacht Owners Association
Box 9997
Yacht Haven Marina
St. Thomas, United States Virgin Islands 00801
(800) 524-2073

Discovery Yacht Charters
15 Water Street E.
Little Current, Ontario P0P 1K0
Canada
(800) 268-8222

International School of Sailing
P.O. Box 9997
St. Thomas, United States Virgin Islands 00801
(809) 774-3677

Island Yachts
6807 Estate Smith Bay
18-B Red Hook Qtr
Charlotte Amalie
St. Thomas, United States Virgin Islands 00802
(800) 524-2019

Latitude 18
Box 88
Red Hook
St. Thomas, United States Virgin Islands 00802
(800) 925-0315

Misty Isle Yacht Charters
Box 1118
Virgin Gorda, British Virgin Islands
(809) 495-5643

Charter Companies

Neptune Charters
Compass Point
St. Thomas, United States
Virgin Islands 00802
(800) 637-6402

Proper Yachts
P.O. Box 70
Cruz Bay
St. John, United States Virgin
Islands 00831
(809) 776-6256

Tortola Marine Management
Norwalk Cove Marina
Beach Road
East Norwalk, Connecticut
06855
(800) 633-0155

Virgin Islands Power Yacht
Charters
P.O. Box 6760
St. Thomas, United States
Virgin Islands 00804
(800) 524-2015

Windward/Leeward Islands

Kiriacoulis Caraibe
2750 Black Rock Turnpike
#85
Fairfield, Connecticut 06430
(800) 635-8895

Nautor's Swan Charters
55 America's Cup Avenue
Newport, Rhode Island 02840
(800) 356-7926

Sun Yacht Charters
P.O. Box 737
Camden, Maine 04843
(800) 772-3500

Trade Wind Yachts
P.O. Box 1186
Gloucester, Virginia 23061
(800) 825-7245

Bahamas

Abaco Bahamas Charters
10905 Cowgill Place
Louisville, Kentucky 40243
(800) 626-5690

Eleuthera-Bahamas Charters
190 Widgeon Drive
Eastham, Massachusetts 02642
(800) 548-9684

Charter Brokers

Ann Wallis White
P.O. Box 4100
Hornpoint Marina
Annapolis, Maryland 21403
(800) 732-3861

Interpac Yachts Inc.
1050 Anchorage Lane
San Diego, California 92106
(619) 222-0327

Lynn Jachney Charters
Box 302
Marblehead, Massachusetts
01945
(800) 223-2050

Ocean Voyages
1709 Bridgeway
Sausalito, California 94965
(415) 332-4681

The Sacks Group
1650 S.E. 17th Street
Fort Lauderdale, Florida
33316
(305) 764-7742

Tom Collins Yachts
400 S. Hibiscus Drive
Miami Beach, Florida 33139
(800) 637-5407

FURTHER READING

General

Harbors of Enchantment, Cynthia Kaul (Waitsfield, Vt.: Concepts Publishing, 1989)
The Sailing Lifestyle, John Rousmaniere (New York: Simon & Schuster, 1985)
World Cruising Handbook, Jimmy Cornell (Camden, Maine: International Marine Publishing, 1991)

Seamanship

The Annapolis Book of Seamanship, John Rousmaniere (New York: Simon & Schuster, 1989)

Safety/First Aid

Advanced First Aid Afloat, Peter F. Eastman, M.D. (Centreville, Md.: Cornell Maritime Press, 1974)
Dr. Cohen's Healthy Sailor Book, Michael Cohen, M.D. (Camden, Maine: International Marine Publishing, 1983)
Medical Emergencies at Sea, William Kessler, M.D. (New York: William Morrow & Co., 1986)
Your Offshore Doctor, Michael H. Beilan, M.D. (New York: Dodd-Mead, 1985)

Caribbean

Caribbean Cruising Handbook, Bill Robinson (New York: Dodd-Mead, 1986)
Cruising Guide: St. Martin, St. Kitts, Nevis (Philadelphia: Virgin Island Plus Yacht Charters, 1990)
Cruising Guide to the Caribbean and Bahamas, Hart & Stone (New York: Dodd-Mead, 1982)
Cruising Guide to the Eastern Caribbean (4 volumes), Don Street (New York: W. W. Norton, 1980)
Cruising Guide to the Leeward Islands (Dunedin, Fla.: Cruising Guide Publications, 1993)
Cruising Guide to the Virgin Islands, Simon Scott (Dunedin, Fla.: Cruising Guide Publications, 1993)
Exploring the Windward Islands (Dunedin, Fla.: Cruising Guide Publications, 1993)
Sailor's Guide to the Windward Islands (Dunedin, Fla.: Cruising Guide Publications, 1991)
Street's Cruising Guides (various editions), Don Street (New York: W. W. Norton)
Yachtsman's Guide to the Virgin Islands, Harry Kline (North Miami, Fla.: Tropic Isle Publishers, 1993)

Bahamas

Bahama Islands, Rigg/Kline (New York: Charles Scribner's Sons, 1986)
Yachtsman's Guide to the Bahamas, Harry Kline (North Miami, Fla.: Tropic Isle Publishers, 1993)

Florida

Cruising Guide to the Florida Keys, Capt. Frank Papy (Minnetonka, Minn.: Publication Arts, 1990)
The Intracoastal Waterway, Jan and Bill Moeller (Camden, Maine: International Marine Publishing, 1985)
Waterway Guide, Southern Edition (Annapolis, Md.: Waterway Guides, 1993)

Great Lakes

Well-Favored Passage, Marjorie Cahn Brazer (Manchester, Mich.: Heron Books, 1985)
Waterway Guide, Great Lakes Edition (Annapolis, Md.: Waterway Guides, 1993)
The Ports Cruising Guide to Georgian Bay and The North Channel (Toronto, Ontario, Canada: Overleaf Design Ltd., 1985)

Chesapeake

Waterway Guide, Mid-Atlantic Edition (Annapolis, Md.: Waterway Guides, 1993)
Cruising Guide to the Chesapeake, Stone & Blanchard (New York: Dodd-Mead, 1983)

Pacific Northwest

Cruising Guides, various editions for Canadian waters (Vancouver, B.C., Canada: Pacific Yachting)
Cruising the San Juan Islands, Bruce Calhoun (Newport Beach, Calif.: Sea Publications, 1973)
Northwest Passages, Bruce Calhoun (Newport Beach, Calif.: Sea Publications, 1972)
The San Juan Islands, Afoot and Afloat, Marge Mueller (Seattle, Wash.: The Mountaineers, 1983)

New England

Cruising Guide to the New England Coast, Robert Duncan & John Warem (New York: Dodd-Mead, 1983)

California

California Coastal Passages, Brian Fagan (Santa Barbara, Calif.: Capra Press, 1981)
Cruising Guide to California's Channel Islands, Brian Fagan (Ventura, Calif.: Western Marine Enterprises, 1983)
Cruising the Delta, Hal Schell (Stockton, Calif.: Schell Books, 1983)
Dawdling on the Delta, Hal Schell (Stockton, Calif.: Schell Books, 1983)

Baja California

Baja Boater's Guide (two volumes), Jack Williams (Sausalito, Calif.: Williams Publications, 1988)

Sea of Cortez Guide, Dix Brow (Ventura, Calif.: Western Marine Enterprises, 1983)

British Isles

The Channel Harbours and Anchorages (London: Adlard Coles, 1992)

Cruising Association Handbook (London: Cruising Association, 1992)

Scottish West Coast Pilot, Mark Brackenbury (London: Stanford Maritime, 1992)

South England Pilot (several volumes), Robin Brandon (Huntingdon, England: Imray, 1993)

Norway

Norwegian Cruising Guide, Mark Brackenbury (London: Adlard Coles, 1992)

Turkey

Cruising Guide to the Turquoise Coasts of Turkey, Marcia Davock (Stamford, Conn.: Wescott Cove Publishing, 1990)

Turkey and the Dodecanese Cruising Pilot, Robin Petherbridge (London: Adlard Coles, 1992)

Greece

Greek Waters Pilot, Rod Heikell (Huntingdon, England: Imray, 1993)

The Aegean: A Sea Guide, H. M. Denham (London: John Murray, 1988)

Mediterranean

Italian Waters Pilot, Rod Heikell (Huntingdon, England: Imray, 1993)

Mediterranean Cruising Handbook, Rod Heikell (Huntingdon, England: Imray, 1993)

South France Pilot, Robin Brandon (Huntingdon, England: Imray, 1993)

South Pacific and Asia

Cruising Guide to the Bay of Islands, Julius Wilensky (Stamford, Conn.: Wescott Cove Publishing, 1985)

Cruising Guide to Tahiti and French Polynesia (Clearwater, Fla.: The Moorings, 1988)

Cruising Guide to Tahiti and French Society Islands, Marcia Davock (Stamford, Conn.: Wescott Cove Publishing, 1985)

Landfalls of Paradise, Earl R. Hinz (Ventura, Calif.: Western Marine Enterprises, 1983)

New Zealand's Bay of Islands: The Land and Sea Guide, Claire Jones (Opua, New Zealand: Port of Opua Trading Co, 1985)

Thailand: Sail Thailand (Bangkok: Artasia Press, 1990)

MAGAZINES

Cruising World (primarily sail)
5 John Clarke Road
Newport, Rhode Island 02840

Motor Boating & Sailing (power and sail)
250 W. 55th Street
New York, New York 10019

Power & Motoryacht (primarily power)
475 Park Avenue S
New York, New York 10016

The Robb Report (primarily mega-yachts)
One Acton Place
Acton, Massachusetts 01720

Sail (primarily sail)
275 Washington Street
Newton, Massachusetts 02158

Sailing (primarily sail)
125 E. Main Street
Port Washington, Wisconsin 53074

Sea (sail and power, western U.S.)
17782 Cowan
Irvine, California 92714

Showboats International (primarily mega-yachts)
1600 SE 17th Street #200
Fort Lauderdale, Florida 33316

CHECKLISTS

CLOTHING AND GEAR TO TAKE WITH YOU

It should be obvious that this list is not complete, and you'll need to determine what clothing you want to suit the area and your cruising plans. Take a wider selection of clothing for cruising in the Pacific Northwest or Northern Europe, where you may have warm, cool, or wet days. For trips to the Caribbean or French Polynesia, you can reduce your wardrobe to reflect a generally warmer and more stable climate. Listed below are items that you might otherwise forget:

Clothing
- ☐ Seabag or duffel bag to carry everything
- ☐ Polarized sunglasses and cord to hold them around the neck
- ☐ Two pairs of boating shoes (one is likely to get wet at some point)
- ☐ Worn-out sneakers for wading or swimming around reefs
- ☐ Two bathing suits, so one can dry while the other is being worn
- ☐ Athletic socks, to prevent blisters from swim fins
- ☐ Sailing hat

Cold or Wet Weather Clothing
- ☐ Watch cap
- ☐ Gloves
- ☐ Scarf

- ☐ Foul-weather jacket and pants
- ☐ Sea boots
- ☐ Wool sweaters
- ☐ Small towel to wrap around the neck

PERSONAL
- ☐ Seasickness pills, ear patches, or wrist straps
- ☐ Sunscreen
- ☐ Lip balm
- ☐ Insect repellent
- ☐ Lomotil (prescription) or Kaopectate antidiarrheal medicine
- ☐ Toilet paper
- ☐ Skin lotion (Avon's Skin So Soft is a good bug repellent)
- ☐ Several small bars of soap
- ☐ Passport, even if not required, to simplify identification
- ☐ Visa for passport if needed
- ☐ Traveler's checks
- ☐ Credit cards
- ☐ Lotion for insect stings
- ☐ Extra prescription medications
- ☐ Hydrogen peroxide or Betadine for coral cuts
- ☐ Extra pair of prescription glasses
- ☐ Eye shades and ear plugs for flying
- ☐ Sketch pad and pencils
- ☐ Diary with blank pages
- ☐ Sewing kit

SAILING GEAR
- ☐ Binoculars
- ☐ Sailing gloves
- ☐ Flashlight, pocket-sized
- ☐ Rigging knife
- ☐ Garden or work gloves for anchoring, to keep off slime and tar
- ☐ Flotation vest

Toys
- [ ] Face mask, snorkel, and swim fins
- [ ] Camera, extra lenses, lots of film, filters, extra batteries, flash
- [ ] Playing cards, two packs
- [ ] Board games such as Scrabble or Monopoly
- [ ] Stereo tape cassettes or CDs
- [ ] Paperback books

Miscellaneous
- [ ] Your yacht-club burgee
- [ ] Electric adapters for your shore stay in foreign countries
- [ ] Binoculars
- [ ] Canvas tote bag
- [ ] Guidebooks to area, local shells, birds, etc.
- [ ] Foreign dictionary/phrase book
- [ ] Plastic bags for holding shells or laundry
- [ ] Matches
- [ ] Clothespins

BAREBOAT CHECKOUT LIST

Checking out on an unfamiliar charter yacht can be useful or frustrating, but the following list offers some suggestions for the information you need to enjoy a pleasant and safe charter:

DECK
- ☐ Anchor windlass operation, amount of rode and chain aboard, location of spare anchor, emergency windlass procedures
- ☐ Location and number of docklines and fenders
- ☐ Location of extra blocks, lines, winch handles
- ☐ Operation of bimini top and cockpit table

SAFETY
- ☐ Location of all life jackets, flares, fire extinguishers
- ☐ Location and use of boarding ladder and man-overboard equipment
- ☐ Operation and location of manual and automatic bilge pumps
- ☐ Location and installation of emergency tiller
- ☐ Test all flash and spotlights

MECHANICAL
- ☐ Location of all thru-hull fittings and operation of seacocks
- ☐ Location of batteries, operation of battery switches

- ☐ Operation of head and shower sump pump
- ☐ Proper methods of checking oil and water in engine
- ☐ Recommended rpm, oil pressure, water temperature
- ☐ Understand all switches and gauges on instrument panel
- ☐ Fuel-tank capacity, location of deck-plate filler
- ☐ Operation of all lights and location of spare bulbs

Galley
- ☐ Operation of stove
- ☐ Location of spare stove fuel canisters and changeover procedure
- ☐ Proper operation of refrigerator/freezer
- ☐ Capacity of water tank, valves for switching tanks, location of deck plate for filling water tank

Dinghy
- ☐ Operation of outboard, proper fuel and oil mixtures, spare shear pin
- ☐ Location of oars, bailer, fuel tank
- ☐ If inflatable, operation of inflation pump

Navigation
- ☐ Location of all charts and cruising guides
- ☐ Proper documentation and ship's papers for customs clearances
- ☐ Proper use of radio (what channel does charter company monitor, channel and time of local weather broadcasts)

General
- ☐ Conversion of dinette to berth
- ☐ Location and count of linens and towels

External
- ☐ Check condition of hull, rub rails, mast and rigging. Note in writing on checkout sheet any gouges or other damage to prevent being charged later.
- ☐ If possible, raise main and unfurl jib at dock to examine condition.
- ☐ Confirm location and count of winch handles.

DAILY CHECKLISTS

Each day you should prepare your charter yacht for use just as a pilot goes through a preflight checklist. The following is a minimum list for a presail inspection:

ENGINE PRESTART
- ☐ Check oil level, coolant level, belts
- ☐ Run blower
- ☐ Note fuel level and record amount used daily

WARMED ENGINE
- ☐ Monitor oil pressure, coolant temp, charging rate
- ☐ Water coming from exhaust

BILGES
- ☐ Check and pump dry daily

FRESH WATER
- ☐ Check and record amount used daily

STREETOVE FUEL
- ☐ Check and record daily

ANCHOR READINESS
- ☐ Make sure primary anchor is ready for instant use

Deck
- ☐ Put away or secure all loose cushions
- ☐ Streetow all personal belongings

Below
- ☐ Close all hatches and ports until at sea
- ☐ Streetow all gear that may fall when boat heels
- ☐ Make sure all lockers and drawers are secured shut

LOCATION INDEX

Abacos Islands, Bahamas, 176–177
Abel Point, Australia, 215
Admiralty Island, Alaska, 189
Adrigold, Ireland, 200
Aegina, Greece, 193
Airlie Beach, Australia, 215
Aland Islands, Finland, 195
Allan's Cay, Exumas, 177
Amsterdam, Netherlands, 201
Anacortes, Washington, 188
Andaman Sea, Thailand, 218
Anguilla, Leeward Islands, 160, 165–166
Annapolis, Maryland, 180
Anse, d'Arlet, Martinique, 168
Anse Mitan, Martinique, 168
Antalya, Turkey, 203–204
Antibes, France, 202
Antigua, Leeward Islands, 167, 172
Apostle Islands, Great Lakes, 20, 186
Argolis Gulf, Greece, 192
Aruba, Caribbean, 160
Astakos, Greece, 194
Athens, Greece, 193
Auckland, New Zealand, 211
Aurray, France, 200
Australia, 214–217
Avalon, California, 187

Bahamas Islands, 174–177
Baie d'Avea, French Polynesia, 207

Baja California, Mexico, 15, 19, 21, 181–182
Balboa Island, California, 187
Bantry Bay, Ireland, 200
Basse-Terre, Guadeloupe, 167
Baths, Virgin Islands, 163
Bay of Islands, New Zealand, 209–211
Bequia, Grenadines, 169
Bimini, Bahamas, 177
Block Island, Rhode Island, 184
Bodrum, Turkey, 203
Bonaire, Dutch Leewards, 160
Bora Bora, French Polynesia, 205–206
Britannia Bay, Grenadines, 170
Brittany, France, 199–200
Bush Key, Florida, 179

Caledonian Canal, Scotland, 197
Canada, 185–186, 188–190
Cane Garden Bay, Virgin Islands, 163
Caneel Bay, Virgin Islands, 164
Cannes, France, 202
Cannouan Island, Grenadines, 170
Cape Brett, New Zealand, 209–210
Cape Cod, Massachusetts, 184
Caribbean, 159–173
Carriacou, Grenadines, 171
Castle Haven, Ireland, 200
Catalina Island, California, 187
Channel Islands, England, 199
Chao Lai, Thailand, 219

Location Index

Charlestown Bay, Grenadines, 170
Charlotte Amalie, Virgin Islands, 164
Chatham Bay, Grenadines, 170
Cherbourg, France, 199
Chesapeake Bay, 179–181
Chestertown, Maryland, 180
Clifton Harbor, Grenadines, 170
Cooper's Islands, Virgin Islands, 164
Cornwall, England, 199
Coromandel Peninsula, New Zealand, 211
Corsica, France, 202
Costa Smeralda, Italy, 203
Cowan Water, Australia, 217
Crosshaven, Ireland, 200
Cruz Bay, Virgin Islands, 164
Curacao, Caribbean, 160

Deep Bay, Antigua, 167
Denmark, 195–196
Devon, England, 199
Dickenson Bay, Antigua, 167
Dodecanese Islands, Greece, 193
Dominica, Leeward Islands, 165, 168
Drake's Anchorage, Virgin Islands, 164
Dry Torgugas, Florida, 179

Eigg, Scotland, 197
Elba, Italy, 203
Eleuthera Island, Exumas, 177
England, 197–199
English Channel, 199
English Harbour, Antigua, 167
Espirtu Santo, Mexico, 181
Exumas Islands, Bahamas, 177–178

Fare, French Polynesia, 207
Faro Blanco, Florida, 178
Finland, 194–196
Five Islands, Antigua, 167
Florida Keys, 178–179

Foeata, Tonga, 213
Fort Lauderdale, Florida, 178
Fort-de-France, Martinique, 168
Fossil Bay, Washington, 189
France, 199–201
Friday Harbor, Washington, 188
Friendship Bay, Grenadines, 169
Fyn, Denmark, 196

Galapagos Islands, 10
Garden Key, Florida, 179
Georgetown, Exumas, 177
Georgian Bay, Great Lakes, 186
Glacier Bay, Alaska, 189
Gorda Sound, Virgin Islands, 163
Grand Bahama Island, Bahamas, 177
Grand Case, St. Martin, 165
Grand-Terre, Guadeloupe, 167
Great Barrier Island, New Zealand, 211
Great Barrier Reef, Australia, 215
Great Guana Cay, Bahamas, 176
Great Lakes, 185–187
Greater Antilles, Caribbean, 160
Greek Islands, 10, 191–194
Green Turtle Cay, Bahamas, 177
Grenada, Grenadines, 169, 171–172
Grenadines, 169
Grynt, Finland, 195
Guadeloupe, Leeward Islands, 165, 167–168
Guernsey, England, 199
Gulf Islands, Canada, 189
Gulf of Bothnia, Finland, 195
Gustavia, Leeward Islands, 166

Hamilton Island, Australia, 215–216
Hango, Finland, 195
Happy Bay, Australia, 215
Hauraki Gulf, New Zealand, 211
Hawk Channel, Florida, 178
Hawkesbury, Australia, 217

Location Index

Hebrides Islands, Scotland, 197
Highbourne Cay, Exumas, 177
Honeymoon Beach, Virgin Islands, 165
Hook Island, Australia, 215
Hoorn, Netherlands, 201
Hope Town, Bahamas, 176–177
Horseshoe Reefs, Grenadines, 170
Huahiné, French Polynesia, 205, 206, 207
Hunga Lagoon, Tonga, 213
Hydra, Greece, 193

Ijsselmeer, Netherlands, 201
Ionian Sea, Greece, 193
Ireland, 200
Isle of Wight, England, 199

James Bond Island, Thailand, 219
Jersey, England, 199
Jervis Inlet, Canada, 189
Jost Van Dyke, Virgin Islands, 164
Juneau, Alaska, 189
Jutland, Denmark, 196

Kalamas, Greece, 193
Kalimnos, Greece, 193
Kalkan, Turkey, 203
Kapa Island, Tonga, 213
Kas, Turkey, 203
Kattegat, Denmark, 196
Kekova, Turkey, 203
Kerikeri, New Zealand, 209–211
Key Largo, Florida, 178
Key West, Florida, 178
Kilarney, Canada, 186
Kingstown, Grenadines, 169
Kinsale, Ireland, 200
Ko Pan Yia, Thailand, 219
Ko Racha Yai, Thailand, 220
Koh Surin, Thailand, 220
Kos, Greece, 193

La Paz, Mexico, 181
Lake Huron, 186
Leeward Islands, Caribbean, 160
Leros, Greece, 193
Les Saintes, Guadeloupe, 168
Lesser Antilles, Caribbean, 160
Levkas, Greece, 193
Limfjord, Denmark, 196
Little Current, Canada, 186
Little Muddy, New Zealand, 211
Loch Ness, Scotland, 197
Locke, California, 183
Long Beach Harbor, California, 187
Long Island Sound, 185
Los Angeles Harbor, California, 187
Lost Slough, California, 183

Madeline Island, Great Lakes, 186
Maine, 184–185
Makkum, Netherlands, 201
Man O'War Bay, New Zealand, 211
Maninita, Tonga, 213
Manitoulin Island, Great Lakes, 186
Man-O-War Cay, Bahamas, 176–177
Marathon, Florida, 178
Marcel Bay, St. Martin, 165
Marigot Bay, St. Lucia, 168
Marigot, St. Martin, 165
Marina del Rey, California, 187
Marmaris, Turkey, 203
Marquesas Keys, Florida, 179
Marsh Harbour, Bahamas, 175
Martinique, Windward Islands, 168
Mayreau, Grenadines, 170
Meadows, the, California, 183
Mechanical failure, 130–131
Mediterranean, 201
Meganisi, Greece, 193
Miami, Florida, 178
Mission Bay, California, 187
Mokelumne River, California, 183
Morbihan, France, 200

Location Index

Mosquito Cove, Antigua, 167
Motorua, New Zealand, 209
Motuarohia, New Zealand, 210
Mount Desert, Maine, 184
Muiden, Netherlands, 201
Muiderslot, Netherlands, 201
Mull, Scotland, 197
Mustique, Grenadines, 169–170
Mystic, Connecticut, 184

Nantucket Island, Massachusetts, 184
Nara Inlet, Australia, 215
Narragansett Bay, 184
Neiafu, Tonga, 213
Netherlands, 201
New Plymouth, Bahamas, 176
New Zealand, 209
Newport Harbor, California, 187
Newport, Rhode Island, 184
Nice, France, 202
Norman Island, Virgin Islands, 163
Normandy, France, 199
North Channel, Great Lakes, 185–186
Norway, 194, 196
Nuapapu Island, Tonga, 213

Omaru, New Zealand, 211
Opito Bay, New Zealand, 211
Opua, New Zealand, 209
Opunga Cove, New Zealand, 210
Orient Bay, St. Martin, 165
Otehei Bay, New Zealand, 210
Oysterhaven, Ireland, 200

Pacific Northwest, 15, 19, 188–190
Palm Bay, Australia, 215
Patmos, Greece, 193
Phang Nga Bay, Thailand, 218–219
Phi Phi Islands, Thailand, 220
Philipsburg, St. Martin, 165
Phuket, Thailand, 218–219
Pigeon Island, Guadeloupe, 168

Pioneer Bay, Australia, 215
Pipi Bay, New Zealand, 209
Piraeus, Greece, 192
Pitons, The, St. Lucia, 168–169
Pittwater, Australia, 217
Plantation Key, Florida, 178
Poros, Greece, 193
Port Bourayne, French Polynesia, 207
Port Fitzroy, New Zealand, 211
Portofino, Italy, 202
Portree, Scotland, 197
Prevost Harbor, Washington, 189
Prickly Bay, Grenada, 171
Prickly Pear Cays, Leeward Islands, 166
Princess Louisa Inlet, Canada, 189
Puget Sound, Washington, 188

Raiatéa, French Polynesia, 205, 206, 208
Red Hook Bay, Virgin Islands, 164
Redon, France, 200
Reid Harbor, Washington, 189
Rhodes, Greece, 203
Rhum, Scotland, 197
Road Bay, Anguilla, 165
Roche Harbor, Washington, 189
Rodney Bay, St. Lucia, 169
Russell, New Zealand, 209, 211

Saba, Leeward Islands, 167
Sacramento Delta, California, 182–183
Salt Island, Virgin Islands, 163
Salt Whistle Bay, Grenadines, 170
Sampson's Cay, Exumas, 177
San Diego, California, 187
San Salvador, Bahamas, 174
Sandy Cay, Anguilla, 166
Sardinia, Italy, 203
Sark, England, 199
Saronic Gulf, Greece, 192
Scandinavia, 194–196

Location Index

Scotland, 15, 21, 197–198
Seattle, Washington, 188
Shute Harbour, Australia, 215
Similan Islands, Thailand, 219
Simpson Bay, St. Martin, 165
Sir Francis Drake Channel, Virgin Islands, 163
Sjaelland, Denmark, 196
Skiathos, Greece, 193
Skopelos, Greece, 193
Skye, Scotland, 197
Skyros, Greece, 193
Smith Island, Maryland, 180
Solent, England, 199
Spa Creek, Maryland, 180
Spetsai, Greece, 193
Sporades Islands, Greece, 193
St. Ann, Martinique, 168
Staniel Cay, Exumas, 177
Strait of Georgia, Canada, 189
Stuart Island, Washington, 189
St. Anna's, Finland, 195
St. Barts, Leeward Islands, 166–167, 172
St. George's, Grenada, 171
St. John, Virgin Islands, 164
St. Kitts, Leeward Islands, 165
St. Lucia, Windward Islands, 168–169
St. Martin, Leeward Islands, 160, 165, 172
St. Michael's, Maryland, 180
St. Thomas, Virgin Islands, 164
St. Tropez, France, 202
St. Vincent, Windward Islands, 169
Sucia Island, Washington, 189
Sweden, 195–196
Sydney, Australia, 217

Tahaa, French Polynesia, 205, 206, 207
Tahiti, 21, 205–209
Tangier Island, Maryland, 180
Te Hue Bay, New Zealand, 209
Te Kouma Harbour, New Zealand, 211
Thailand, 15, 217–220
Tobago Cays, Grenadines, 170
Tonga, 212–214
Tortola, Virgin Islands, 162–163
Treasure Cay, Bahamas, 176
Turkey, 203
Turks Islands, Bahamas, 174
Turku, Sweden, 195
Turtle Bay, Australia, 216
Two Harbors, California, 187
Tyrell Bay, Grenadines, 171

Union Island, Grenadines, 170

Vancouver Island, Canada, 189
Vannes, France, 200
Vastervik, Finland, 195
Vava'u, Tonga, 213
Virgin Gorda, Virgin Islands, 163
Virgin Islands, 12, 20, 28, 161–165
Vixen Point, Virgin Islands, 164
Volendam, Netherlands, 201

Wadden Zee, Netherlands, 201
Waiheke, New Zealand, 211
Whangamamumu Harbor, New Zealand, 210
Whitehaven Beach, Australia, 216
Whitsunday Islands, Australia, 214–216
Windward Islands, Caribbean, 160
World's End Reef, Grenadines, 170

Xanthus, Turkey, 203

Zeeland, Netherlands, 201
Zuiderzee, Netherlands, 201

TOPIC INDEX

Anchors and anchoring, 44, 100–110

Bahamas mooring style, 110
Barbecues, 153
Bareboating, 5–6
Bites and stings, 134–135
Breakdowns, 29
Bugs, 154–155

Catamarans, 40
Charter boats, size, 37
Charter brokers, 26–27, 71–72, 79
Charter companies, choosing a, 25
Charter costs, 20
Charter paperwork, booking, 51–52
  cancellations, 53
  clearance, 151
  contracts, 57, 75
  deposits, 51
  insurance, 54–56
  inventory, 57
  sailing résumé, 52
  security deposit, 54
Charter problems, miscellaneous, 56–57
Charter rates, sample, 16–17, 75–76, 80
Charter seasons, 22–23
Charter yachts, equipment, 44, 46
  layout, 38–40
  privacy aboard, 43
  racing, 172–173
Charters, crewed, 6, 69–80
Charters, experience required, 20
Charters, flotilla, 7
Charters, head boats, 11
Charters, types of, 5
Check-in procedures, 59–60
Check-out procedures, 92–93, 117–118
Children aboard, 77, 155–156
Classification societies, 73
Clothing, what to take, 81–84
Coast Guard licenses, 33, 72
Collision, 128–129
Credit cards, 54, 56, 88
Crew overboard, 124–125
Crewed charter terms, 74–75
Crewed charters, 6–7, 69–80
Crew, choosing a, 47–50
Cruising limits, 28

Damage report, 58
Demise charter terms, 75
Dinghies, 46, 117–122
Docking and undocking, 93–95

Emergencies, crew overboard, 124–125
  fire, 125–126
  flooding, 127–128

Emergencies (*cont.*)
   mechanical failure, 130–131
   medical, 135
   running aground, 126–127
   wrapped prop, 129–130

Fire, 125–126
First aid, 131–135
   bites and stings, 134–135
   seasickness, 87, 133–134
   serious trauma, 135
   sunburn, 132–133
Flags, courtesy, 151–152
Flooding, 127–128
Flotilla charters, 7–9

Galleys, 46, 63–64
Generators, 65, 154Insurance, 54–56

Knots, basic, 98–99

Logbook, 58
Luggage and duffel bags, 53, 81

Mechanical failure, 130–131
Mediterranean mooring style, 106–110
Money, 152
Mooring buoys, 96

Navigation, tools, 114–116

Old Boy Network, 31
Outboards, 118, 121–122

Paperwork, clearance papers, 151
Photographic equipment and film, 53, 84–85, 120
Powerboat charters, 61–68
Protocol, crewed charter, 76–78
Provisioning, 136–146
   sample menus, 144–146

Radio procedures, 116, 126, 128–129, 135
Reefing, 97–98
Refrigerators, 149

Sailing schools, 9, 23
Seasickness, 87, 133–134
Skippers, rates, 6
Storage, 150
Sunburn, 132–133
Sunglasses, polarized, 85

Taxes, 21
Tipping, 78
Toilet, 148

Ventilation, 42

Water, fresh, 42–43, 147–148
Western Med. terms, 74